A
MOMENT'S
PAUSE
from the
SPOKEN WORD

given by
J. Spencer Kinard

Deseret Book Company
Salt Lake City, Utah

Library of Congress Catalog Card No. 89-40408
ISBN 0-87579-248-0

Printed in the United States of America
10   9   8   7   6   5   4   3   2   1

Published by Deseret Book Company
P.O. Box 30178, Salt Lake City, Utah 84130

Contents

MOMENTS OF GROWTH

MOMENTS OF CHANGE

MOMENTS OF GRATITUDE

MOMENTS WITH FAMILY

MOMENTS WITH FRIENDS

MOMENTS OF BROTHERHOOD

MOMENTS WITH THE SAVIOR

Foreword

Expressions of inspiration that are succinct and poignant are rare in today's cluttered world. Providing meaningful messages to a widely diversified audience without inciting controversy or giving offense is the weekly challenge of J. Spencer Kinard.

The "word" has been part of the broadcast of "Music and the Spoken Word" for most of its sixty years. The process through which the brief messages are created has remained a very personal matter. Spencer works with a staff of excellent producers, directors, and writers, but in the end he, with his own unique ability and personality, judges, edits, and molds these vignettes into life. His talented delivery and his genuineness as a man are the catalysts that invest his sermonettes with strength and credibility.

In written form, too, as they appear here, these unique word capsules express a consistent faith in the worth of mankind for every person in general from the spirit of one person in particular.

JEROLD OTTLEY

Acknowledgments

The responsibility for creating the weekly message known as "The Spoken Word" falls to several people. Bonneville Media Communications producer Ed Payne assigns a writer to a given week. The five writers who share the rotating assignment for each week's script are Ray Haeckel, Duane Hiatt, Clifton Jolley, Maurine Proctor, and Michael Robinson. The draft of the script is given to Carroll Smith, of BMC, to retype and send to me to edit or rewrite. To each of these people and many others who share the creativity, the labor, and the joy of this weekly endeavor, I give my thanks.

J. SPENCER KINARD

MOMENTS
OF
FAITH

The Faith of a Mustard Seed

Developing the power of faith is one of the most important phases of our experience in mortal life. In order to do the things that are best for us, we must believe we are capable.

Faith can motivate us, give us a positive approach to living, give us the desire to improve ourselves. It's interesting to observe that where one person is defeated by a handicap, another is stimulated; where one complains about hardship, another fights against it; where one is paralyzed by disaster, another rises to the challenge. Faith and attitude make the difference.

Faith in the future can cause positive things to happen in our lives. Faith in ourselves will help us develop the right kind of self-image to keep our habits, lives, and souls headed in the proper direction. Without faith in God, life will burden the heart, the mind, and even the soul.

Certainly, faith is affected by our experiences. There is usually a time in life when our "faith line" hits bottom. That's when we must decide either to continue the decline or to force an upturn. The challenge usually comes during early adulthood when we come face-to-face with the demands of life and the need for certain material goods and when we become more aware of the weaknesses and strengths of those around us. All of these experiences can build or destroy our faith.

Faith is probably the greatest undeveloped resource in the world. We all have more of it than we may suppose. It's a force that comes from within. It's the power of belief and of conviction.

The Savior spoke of the transcendent power manifest through

the exercise of faith. "If ye had faith as a grain of mustard seed," he said, "ye might say unto this sycamine tree, Be thou plucked up by the root, and be thou planted in the sea; and it should obey you." (Luke 17:6.)

Our challenge is to gain, to increase, to perfect our faith, so that we might have power to uproot sycamine trees, to move mountains, to work miracles, indeed, to realize the worthy goals and objectives we've set for ourselves. The apostle Matthew promised, as recorded in the New Testament, that "all things, whatsoever ye shall ask in prayer, believing, ye shall receive." (Matthew 21:22.) That promise is available to all of us if we anchor our lives on the rock of faith.

Believing Takes Us Home

Recently a film critic for a major metropolitan newspaper criticized a movie for its many "artistic and technical failures." He had little trouble pointing out the technical failures, because there was a standard by which to judge them—exposure, editing, lighting, and so forth. But while it was simple for the critic to point out the technical failures of the film, it was, to the same degree, difficult for him to explain why it failed as art.

Why did so learned an observer have such trouble? Because art concerns itself not only with what we *know* but also with what we *believe,* and not only with what we believe about art but also with what we believe about the world and ourselves.

So it is with our lives. Much of what we do is founded on our knowledge of the world—on what we presume to be facts. We get gas for the car, because we see from the gauge that the tank is nearly empty. Most of the time the evidence is accurate, and our knowledge is sound. But sometimes we are mistaken— sometimes the gauge says there is gas, but the car runs out anyway.

When the evidence does not square with the facts, we might do well to remember that there are other forms of knowledge, other sources of information, other ways to be guided. We might remember a mother's intuition, the grace of a gospel message, or the instinct we have felt to do the right thing in the face of wrong persuasions.

How many times has a mother told her child, "I don't know how I know, but I know"? How many times has a child marveled that, against all possibility of coincidence or discovery, a father or mother has been *inspired* to know the truth—and, more than merely to know it, to act upon it? How many times have we sensed what to do, believed beyond our ignorance, acted in the right way when we had little physical evidence to guide us?

In such instances, what we believe, what we feel, and what a still, small, heavenly voice whispers to us, are more essential and more useful than what we know. Indeed, it is what we *cannot* know that makes belief so important. When the evidences fail— when the facts are inadequate to inspire our knowledge—it is believing that takes us home.

The Power to Be Personal

Most religious music deals with our relationship with the Lord. "I waited for the Lord," we sing. "He inclined unto me. He heard my complaint." While we may sing of these things, do we really believe they are so? Does the Lord, in fact, hear our complaints—both our significant and our sometimes petty human problems? Can the being who created the universe be bothered with the pitiful lament of a lonely soul on a tiny world on the edge of this galaxy?

The answer is yes. But it is easy to feel insignificant before the Lord, even though he has assured us that is not how he feels toward us. The Lord said, "Call unto me, and I will answer thee, and shew thee great and mighty things, which thou knowest not." (Jeremiah 33:3.) It does not diminish the divinity of God to believe that he can incline toward the least of his creations. Quite the contrary—God hears and empathizes with us not in spite of his greatness but because of it, because his is a godly greatness founded on eternal principles of infinite love.

True it is that he has all power. But let us not equate that power with the puffed up pomposity and arrogance that too often accompany earthly power. He does not wield the scepter of power to enlarge his own importance and satisfy his own vanity, as we so often do. He uses his power and knowledge only to bless us; his chief concerns are those he created in his own image—you and me and all mankind.

Yet, he also gives us our agency. God's omniscient knowledge and all-seeing eye are not used to pry into our lives and to control us like puppets on a string. His knowledge and infinite wisdom are brought to bear only on our behalf and only when we're willing to accept them. He sends his Holy Spirit to enlighten our minds, to "show [us] great and mighty things," as the prophet Jeremiah wrote. God uses his knowledge wisely to govern the universe in ways that will best bless his children. He patiently listens to our complaints and gently succors us in our sorrows. It is because God is so powerful, so wise, and so good that he can number the very hairs of our head and, as Jesus said, take note of the lilies of the field and a fallen sparrow. He has the capacity, the organizational abilities, the resources, and, most of all, the fatherly concern for his children to make such individual attention possible.

To know the true nature of God and our relationship with him is the basis of our comfort and happiness here and our glory and exaltation hereafter. Little wonder, then, that we sing hosannas to his name. As we face the challenges of today and the ultimate judgment halls of tomorrow, we should not—we need not—fear, for we have more than a friend at the court. We are sons and daughters of the King himself.

Courage for the Long Haul

The world is full of people who meant to be more than they are, but something happened along the way. They say things just didn't work out or there were too many distractions. They will admit it was harder than they thought or life knocked them to their knees. Excuses abound, but what one rarely hears is, "I didn't have the courage."

We think of courage for the battlefield, courage in the face of a terminal illness. We think of courage for the explorer who is breaking trails into new territory. Courage is one of the most important qualities of daily life, for, in reality, with each sunrise there isn't one of us who isn't breaking trails into new territory. Tomorrow is darkness. We do not know what it will bring.

Perhaps that is why it is so much easier to cling timidly to the familiar, to our own little well-worn grooves, rather than to stretch beyond them. It is easier to walk, sheeplike, along the trails tried by others, rather than turn along our own path. Safety may seem more appealing than real success.

Sidney Smith wrote: "A great deal of talent is lost in the world for want of a little courage. Every day sends to their graves men whom timidity prevented from making a first effort; who, if they could have been induced to begin, would in all probability have gone great lengths in the career of fame. The fact is that to do anything in the world worth doing, we must not stand back shivering and thinking of the cold and danger but jump in and scramble through as well as we can. It will not do to be perpetually calculating risks and adjusting nice chances; . . . at present a man waits, and doubts, and consults his brother, and his particular friends, till one day he finds he is sixty years old and that he has lost so much time in consulting cousins and friends that he has no more time to follow their advice."[1]

The Lord did not place us here to be timid, frightened creatures. He did not mean for us to cling to our place, mere shadows of ourselves. Thus, he made us a promise to give us the courage we would need to cross into our own promised lands.

The Lord told Joshua to be strong and of a good courage. He gave him the reason why he could: "For the Lord thy God is with thee whithersoever thou goest." (Joshua 1:9.) So, also, is the promise for us. With such a companion, who need ever fear?

Facing Fear

Life is a high-risk endeavor. The stakes are enormous. Utter happiness or total heartbreak often depends merely on a difference in a step, a turn of the head, an offhand decision. Misery may suddenly break upon our heads out of nowhere. We may put on shows of confidence for one another, occasional acts of bravado, but it is only the untruthful who never admit to fear. The rest of us are always somewhere between comfortable security and fearful anxiety.

And when at times we are faced with uncertainty, frightened feelings might arise. A full stomach may not please us today if we are not sure of tomorrow's meal. But even in times of relative security, we can never forget how frail is the heart that beats in the person we love most, how limited is our time together. We can never forget in our times of relative confidence how little we know, how prone to error. Pascal said, "Man is but a reed — the weakest thing in nature. . . . It is not necessary that the whole universe should arm itself to crush him. A vapor, a drop of water is enough to kill him."[2]

When life does have its panicky moments, how do we survive them?

Eleanor Roosevelt said, "You gain strength, courage, and confidence by every experience in which you really stop to look fear in the face. You are able to say to yourself, 'I lived through this horror. I can take the next thing that comes along.' The danger lies in refusing to face the fear, in not daring to come to grips with it. If you fail anywhere along the line, it will take your confidence. You must do the thing you cannot do."[3]

When we flee those things that cause us fear, we learn to shrink from life, always waiting for the blow. We end up with a thousand troubles — most of them imaginary. But when we face our fears head-on, a remarkable thing happens. Because *we* don't shrink, our *fears* do. They become manageable, less horrible. In fact, they may become our schoolmasters, teaching us in a marvelous way our strengths, our resiliency, our ability to look anything in the face and say, "I will not let this beat me."

Bit by bit, as we face our fears instead of fleeing before them, we learn that "the only thing we have to fear," as another Roosevelt said, "is fear itself."[4]

Believing in Jesus Christ

On a stormy night, when a wild wind whipped branches off trees and pushed dark clouds across the sky, a frightened little girl cried from her bed for her parents.

And, of course, they came — to comfort her and tell her everything would be all right. "Don't be afraid. It's only the wind."

But the little girl was still afraid. She knew it was the wind, and it was the wind that frightened her. "What *is* the wind?" she cried.

Her father began to explain to her, only to realize that he couldn't. The explanations he knew were about atmospheric conditions, none of which she understood, and she remained frightened.

The wind became more violent, rattling the windows, slamming the garden gate. As the young girl continued to seek comfort, her mother pointed out that the wind not only slams the gate and pulls branches off trees but also "holds your kite in the sky. Would you like to go kite flying tomorrow?"

As the girl continued clinging to her father, not easily persuaded, her mother spoke of the ducks on the pond and the balloon vendor in the park where they would go to fly the kite. Slowly, image by beautiful image, the child followed her mother away from her fear and fell asleep.

Many things in life are difficult to understand. Sometimes the world is too complex to comprehend, and the explanations more confounding than comforting. We are finite creatures, our understanding bounded in the beginning by birth and in the end by death, which is why the infinite eludes us. We are more certain of the effects than the causes, which is why we can count the broken branches but not explain the wind.

Such limitation and ignorance are at once our burden and our blessing. Because we do not understand, we are frightened. And because we are frightened, we are led to Christ and the comfort of a heavenly home. "Except ye be converted," Jesus said, "and become as little children, ye shall not enter into the kingdom of heaven." (Matthew 18:3.) What we do not know is a necessary part of our conversion; what frightens us also returns us to Christ.

In Jesus, we become children again, children who may not yet understand but who are capable of believing in a world whose wind not only slams the gate on a dark night but also pushes the kite against a bright sky.

The Evening of Our Fear

The scriptures speak of faith and the courage that it inspires. Indeed, those who have faith in Christ need fear no final disaster, no ultimate failure. His atoning sacrifice guarantees us that if we will be faithful, he will overcome the tragedy of the moment. He will deliver us out of trouble into the keeping of his salvation and ultimate peace.

But sometimes it is difficult for faith in the future to inspire courage in the present.

Many years ago a young boy, swimming in a public pool, cut his foot on a piece of broken glass on the bottom of the pool. It was a serious wound, leaving a two-inch gash across the ball of his foot.

The wound was painful but not so painful as the boy's fear. It was not a fear of infection or of punishment but of stitches. He looked at the gaping slash, and he imagined the pain of the suture. And the remedy was more fearful to him than the wound.

So he elected not to tell his parents of the trouble. He bound the foot as best he could and hoped for it to heal. It did, but it healed open — leaving what doctors call a plantar scar.

Years later the boy, now a man, remembers the moment of his wounding and the decision inspired by his fear. "When I go barefoot," he says with a wry smile, "that old wound breaks open again. I've tried to have it repaired now that I am past my fear of stitches, but doctors tell me I'm better living with the trouble I caused than possibly causing worse. Surgery at this late date," the man sadly recognizes, "might actually produce a scar more painful than the one I have."

The scar is a relatively minor inconvenience to the man.

More important is the lesson it has taught him: eventually we must face our fear, and the confrontation grows only more terrible as we procrastinate the moment. Wounds that might be treated and healed deepen into scars; scars that would be imperceptible blemishes become more painful afflictions. The soul of a man is not like the sole of a boy's foot: healing always is possible but it is more difficult with the years.

Faith is not easy, nor are its remedies without sacrifice. Indeed, for faith to be active in our lives, we must take courage in its power. But the glory of faith is that it not only requires courage but also gives it. And that same Savior who requires the courage of our faith will bless our faith with courage, and, in the evening of our fear, he will abide with us.

The Conquest of Scarecrows

In America's rural past, farmers used scarecrows in their fields. Timid birds, seeing the cross-sticks attired with an old coat and perhaps a hat, were frightened from an easy meal.

To be sure, the inanimate mannequins were lifeless, crude, and harmless — except to the birds, whose fears brought the scarecrows to life, endowed them with malicious intentions, and gave them power.

And man's own fears are scarecrows that guard the human harvest he might reap.

Without exception, each of us is acquainted with fear — the object and the intensity may vary, but the emotion is the same.

It is fear that stands between us and the realization of our aspirations and ambitions. We lose the possibility of new and self-fulfilling employment because fear ties us to the security of our old job. We shun vocational training and educational opportunities because we fear possible academic failure. The enrichment of new-fledged friends is lost for lack of social courage.

In much that we do — in our work, our studies, our play — we stick to the harbor, afraid of the depths, intimidated by the scarecrows from within, while other, more venturous souls strike for deep water and learn that only fear itself is to be feared, that once fear is conquered, all else may be conquered.

It is true: he who fears will never taste success, while he who conquers fears will never face total defeat. Thus, success is not granted to those who know no fear but to those who overcome their fear, to those wise individuals who dare approach whatever scarecrows haunt the conscious field of self, who disregard the dreaded phantom and even perch upon its spectral head.

In more tangible terms, overcoming our fears is a risky business but one that leads to outward success and inward peace of mind. In fact, it usually turns out that the most fearful of all things is fear itself, even more fearful than that which is feared. We dread going to the dentist, only to learn that the anxiety of anticipation is much worse than the actual visit. We are afraid of old age but then discover that the fear of age is a malady that affects only the young. Even the fear of death is diminished as death approaches.

Using valor and unwavering belief in divine love and protection, let us strike down the scarecrows that haunt us. Stand face to face with fear. With courage and with faith, attack the hideous face of fear.

The Risk of Life

Rudyard Kipling, in a poem titled simply "If," investigates the many attributes of maturity. Among the attributes he discovers, one recurs in several forms: the courage to take risks — not the risks of the gambling hall but of the life lived faithfully and well.

Perhaps risk does not seem a proper description of the faithful life, because there is a certainty in faith, a certainty more substantial than any of the supposed guarantees that the faithless life can offer. But faith does require a leap, an extension of oneself, a risk.

The apostles of Christ were defined by their willingness to take such a risk. When Jesus called to Peter and Andrew on the shores of the Sea of Galilee to "follow me, and I will make you fishers of men," they did not count the costs, or weigh the risks. The scriptures say, "They straightway left their nets, and followed him." (Matthew 4:19–20.)

How unlike the man who inquired of Christ, "What shall I do that I may inherit eternal life?" When the Savior responded that he, like the apostles, must be willing to forsake his wealth, that he must take up the cross, that he must extend himself to follow his Lord, the man went away, unable to risk such sacrifice. (Mark 10:17.)

But is faith really a risk? In the final analysis, it may be the only certainty, the only assurance in life. We may prepare ourselves against disaster, and yet disaster may come, more terrible than any of our preparations can protect us against. We may make wise investments, only to find that the chances of life turn our wisest decisions to foolishness.

Only by risking faith, only by accepting faith in Christ, are all other risks overcome and life made certain. The confidence of the faithful is that whatever the temporary affliction, there will be healing; whatever the calamity, there will be calm, as Kipling wrote:

> If you can dream — and not make dreams your master;
> If you can think — and not make thoughts your aim;
> If you can meet with Triumph and Disaster
> And treat those two imposters just the same. . . .
> . . . .
> If you can fill the unforgiving minute
> With sixty seconds' worth of distance run,
> Yours is the Earth and everything that's in it.

And, we would add, if you can risk faith, even the faith of Christ, then you can put all other risks aside.

Fear

All creatures of the earth seem to be born with some natural instinct that makes them recoil from danger. Rabbits tremble, birds keep frantic watch, and even newborn human infants howl if they think they are about to fall. Fear is an alarm system that keeps us from danger, and only a fool would never admit to occasionally feeling it. George Washington was quoted after a skirmish in 1754 with the French and Indians as saying that bullets whistling past had a "charming sound." When asked about it years later he said, "If I ever said so, I was young."[5] Sometimes our youth or inexperience keeps us from knowing the good of a warning fear.

Conversely, sometimes our fear can keep us from experiencing the good in life. There is always the possibility for human beings that fear can expand beyond its beneficial function and become a menace in itself. That is when fear, like a childhood scar, becomes a permanent part of life, when worry about some impending responsibility, some task yet to do, some future insecurity walks with us much of the time.

Now, some may indulge in worry about a job they have to do because they imagine worrying makes them more responsible, as if anxiety were a key to success in any worthwhile endeavor. Others worry about the well-being of friends and family, believing worrying proves they are more loving. In fact, the fear that edges into worry may be the most futile and debilitating of human emotions.

Anxiety tends to paralyze us, tarnishing our talents and squelching our strengths. This irrational nagging about what might happen makes it so we can do less to determine what will happen. We become frozen before our tasks, fearing that we will not live up to our best capabilities. We procrastinate in the face of challenge, always asking, "Will I do it adequately? Will it all come out right?"

Anxiety also makes us lose the joy of the very moment in which we are alive. One writer observed, "Fear of misfortune is worse than misfortune itself."[6] And so it is. We may find we have spent a lifetime worrying about something that never came to pass.

The Apostle Paul said that the fear and worry that blight us are not from God, "for God hath not given us the spirit of fear; but of power, and of love, and of a sound mind." (2 Timothy 1:7.)

For every human being, the future is as uncertain and dark as the pavement ahead of a blind man; it's that way for all of us. But with the Lord as our light, we need not live anxiously.

Trust in the Lord

A story in the Old Testament tells of the time when the children of Israel were going into fierce battle against the Midianites. There were thirty-two thousand Israelites against an unnumbered host of enemy. The odds looked pretty good for the Israelites. Then the Lord did an unusual thing. He commanded Gideon, the Israelite leader, to reduce the size of the army to only three hundred. What those three hundred must have thought as they watched thousands of their compatriots returning home! What anxieties must have filled their minds the night before they were to meet a host rushing at them with swords!

The Lord's purpose was straightforward in this. He wanted Israel to know with assurance who was winning the battle for them. It wasn't their numbers, their strength, or their prowess. It was the Lord.

"Trust in the Lord with all thine heart," says Proverbs, "and lean not unto thine own understanding." (Proverbs 3:5.)

And it is not an easy lesson. Our agendas are not his agendas; our timetables are not his. Our thoughts are caught in the here and now. Our perspective is limited.

We seek to push our lives along by the power of our own will. But the Lord asks instead that his will, not ours, be done.

Though it sometimes seems nearly impossible, the message is to trust in the Lord. Trust that he hears our prayers and will move our lives along according to a plan designed to make us ultimately most happy. Trust that we don't need to keep all of our problems in our own uncertain hands but can pass them to him with assurance that they will be tended and finally solved.

Trust to the degree that we thrust out the doubt and fear that gnaw at our souls, diminish our dreams, and neutralize our efforts.

Trust in him. And we have every reason to trust. It is the

very Creator of the universe, whose power is unlimited and un-matched, who deigns to call us his own, who asks us to trust, whose devotion to us is undeviating, who hears even the un-spoken yearnings of our souls.

He asks us to trust him, because only when we do, can we live with joy and personal power. Only through trust in God can we move beyond being a "mere bundle of wavering thoughts and fluctuating sensations"[7] to stand on the sure ground of faith and hope and joy in the present and the future.

Faith, Memory, and Patience

Life can be much sweeter if we fully understand the attributes of God. He is love itself, plenteous in mercy, unceasing in his care for us. The mountains rise and fall, but he does not change. Not a hair on our heads is unnoticed by him. "Consider the lilies of the field, how they grow . . . " he said.

"But I say unto you that Solomon in all his glory was not arrayed like one of these.

"Wherefore if God so clothe the grass of the field . . . , how much more will he not provide for you, if ye are not of little faith?" (JST Matthew 6:28–30.)

Provide for us if we have faith. How comforting that sounds in a world that so often pummels us. In a world of light and shadow, the Lord is the one consistency. In that, we can place our faith.

But if our faith sometimes wavers, it may be because two other attributes in us are weak—patience and memory. Faith will falter until it is shored up by these.

Why memory? Because we mortals can be foolish creatures. It is easy for the present to seem eternally upon us. When we are joyous, we can hardly remember trial. The mother, having forgotten labor, gladly goes to childbirth again. And the converse is also true. When we writhe in pain, we think it eternal. We forget that it will pass. We forget that mortal life is like a tide with ebbs and flows, sometimes in the water gasping for air, some-times on the beach in the sunshine.

Faith remembers. Faith is the bird that senses the light and sings while the dawn is still dark.

True faith has a cumulative effect. When the children of Israel stood at the Red Sea and the armies of Egypt came pounding behind them, they could not remember their other miracles in the desert and cried that they had been forgotten.

Faith knows that since God loved and blessed me yesterday, even if I don't feel him today, he still loves and blesses me.

With our remembrance, faith also demands patience, because we see so little here. We are like actors on a dark stage, standing in a spotlight. We cannot see before us. We cannot see what stands in the wings on either side. We stand in our little circle of light and wonder. And, knowing so little, we want things now. We want them on our time schedule. We are restive against God's steady hand and timelessness. But faith accepts God's time frame and comforts us about the future.

With memory and patience, faith can be made whole. No matter what life brings us, we can take advantage of that promise so often repeated in scripture: Ask and ye shall receive. (See Matthew 7:7.)

The Search for Peace

Throughout the scriptures the Lord is continually giving reassurance of his love, his support, and his availability to us at all times.

And when it sometimes seems that we are abandoned during the trials of life or when sorrow and disappointment, failure and weakness make us feel less than we really are, we have access to the healing salve of God's unreserved love.

In the New Testament, the Lord says, "Come unto me, all ye that labour and are heavy laden, and I will give you rest. Take my yoke upon you, and learn of me; for I am meek and lowly in heart: and ye shall find rest unto your souls. For my yoke is easy, and my burden is light." (Matthew 11:28–30.)

That is the Lord's invitation to each of us. And if we accept, it will make a greater difference in our life than anything we have imagined. We will have his comforting influence, the quiet assurances he sends to us. We will give him an opportunity to restore us. The Lord is our most faithful friend. He will never abandon us if we trust him.

His invitation is also a promise of peace. In today's society, it seems that people are more hurried and restless than ever before. Some say it is the result of living in a complex world. But it's more than that. It's the continuing search for inner peace. And after years of dead-end streets, many are returning to chapels and churches to find the peace "which passeth all understanding." (Philippians 4:7.) They have learned that indifference to his influence brings only inner turmoil.

And to those who have felt an emptiness and a loss of perspective, may we suggest that they consider a return to regular weekly worship of the Lord—even as an experiment. The scriptures tell us that "whosoever shall put their trust in God shall be supported in their trials, and their troubles, and their afflictions." (Alma 36:3.)

We must be aware of our continuing need for God and of the fact that we are totally dependent upon him. Let us give the Lord a chance to strengthen us, to enrich our lives, to improve our spiritual stamina, to make our time on earth more meaningful. And what more assuring comfort can we obtain in life than to know that we have established a personal, permanent relationship with God?

The Gift of Faith

In order to do the things that are best for us, we must believe we are capable of doing them. We must have faith. If we excuse ourselves from acting positively because we lack faith in our own abilities, then we are doomed to a passive, negative, and unhappy existence. Faith is the power of the subconscious, of imagining, believing, and convincing ourselves that something can be done.

Thomas Edison once said, "We don't know what electricity is. We don't know what heat is. We have a lot of hypotheses about these things, but that is all. But we do not let our ignorance about these things deprive us of their use." So it is with faith.

All of us have more faith than we sometimes suppose. Every time we plow and plant, we show faith. It is by faith that we build for the future. All of us have doubts at the beginning of a project, but we begin nevertheless.

So, where do this faith and belief come from? They come from within ourselves. Faith is the foundation of commitment. And without commitment, there can be no real progress. The person who has developed the gift of faith is willing to venture boldly into the unknown.

Faith is the key to unlock the door of success, a power that everyone has, but few use it consciously. Those who do are generally optimistic. They are prevention-oriented. Their thoughts focus on wellness, on health, and on success.

Faith is important in all we do. It permeates our existence. We need to have scientific faith, faith in our country, faith in mankind, faith in our children, and faith in eternity.

Perhaps the most important use of this vital gift is to exercise faith in ourselves and faith in God. Surely, everyone, deep in his or her own heart, has some degree of faith in God. Even professed atheists express faith at times. Many say that because they do not understand God or cannot see him, they will not accept him. Yet, they neither see nor hear nor feel many things and still believe in their existence.

Faith can be a moving principle in our lives — a principle of power, of growth, and of real freedom. It is a principle that all may acquire. And if it is not now in your possession, it can be obtained through earnest prayer to him who is the giver of all good gifts.

MOMENTS
OF
TRIAL

A Positive Influence

Trials, troubles, and sorrow are part of our common lot. And as one challenge ends, another seems to quickly take its place. Although God could eliminate our difficulties, he doesn't often do so, because he knows that trials are usually the best stimulus and discipline of celestial character.

What the Lord does give us is relief. When we seek his help, he gives us the strength to bear the burden: he lightens the load. He can make a fifty-pound sack feel like five pounds. And, thus, he is still able to accomplish his purposes. It's a principle best learned early in life.

Probably the worst kind of adversity is a life that's too easy, with too much security, because then we tend to drift and lose our way. There is wisdom in giving us the opportunity to rise above adversity, to try our souls through sorrow. Without adversity, there would be no test of strength, no developing of character, no growth of our personal powers. It's all part of our earthly education, just as the sufferings of the Savior were part of his.

The key to endurance is the development of a strong relationship with the Lord. It will bring stability and a quiet consistency into our lives, even in the face of tribulation. This religious commitment will consistently color our attitude toward everything that happens to us. We won't be shaken, overwhelmed, or frightened by every wind of change. Instead, our spiritual anchor will help insulate us against the buffetings of adversity.

In a positive sense, facing difficulty from time to time is healthy. It forces us to search our hearts. It brings renewed perspective and can provide valuable spiritual insights. It helps us keep our humility and preserves us from pride. It also teaches patience and promotes the deepest as well as the most exalted thought.

So, even though we may become discouraged at times from the obstacles and tests that come to us, we need to remember that the inner peace that comes from keeping God's commandments makes the yoke light. Sometimes that's a hard lesson to learn.

"You'll Never Walk Alone"

If we could have our way, we would book ourselves a safe passage through this life. What day, after all, would we ever choose to face terminal illness, the loss of our dearest love, the winds of adversity or failure? When would we say, "This day I choose pain. Today I choose disappointment"? No day. Yet, the solemn reality is that life will bring us experiences we would never choose, and we are left with that awesome encounter—the revealing of our own character.

Spencer W. Kimball said, "Now, we find many people critical when a righteous person is killed, a young father or mother is taken from a family, or when violent deaths occur. Some become bitter when oft-repeated prayers seem unanswered. . . . But if all the sick were healed, if all the righteous were protected and the wicked destroyed, the whole program of the Father would be annulled and the basic principle of the Gospel, free agency, would be ended."[8]

Pain and sorrow do not immediately follow sin, nor does reward come instantly upon the heels of righteousness. If it did, no one would ever be good simply to be good.

Life will always have sharp edges. The ground will not be soft when we fall on it; viruses will not lose their potency when they near us. So, what are we to make of it all? How are we to wend our way happily in a world so potentially dangerous?

24

Be assured that we can do the things we must. The great message of the gospel is that we don't need to do them alone. We are in the Lord's hands, and what better place to be than in those hands pierced with the nails? Who can hold us more gently against the storm?

The happy ones of this earth are not those free of trial. Hardship is blind, and comes to all. The happy ones are those who know where to seek comfort when the rain falls.

Thomas Carlyle said, "For man's well-being, Faith is properly the one thing needful; how, with it, Martyrs, otherwise weak, can cheerfully endure the shame and the cross; and without it, Worldlings puke-up their existence, by suicide, in the midst of luxury."[9]

Misery need not make us miserable. The sharpest pain can be blunted and turned to peace. When you choose to put your hand in the Lord's, though the storm blows, you'll never walk alone.

Enduring to the End

To endure to the end is the charge given us throughout the scriptures. As we pause to honor those who have already endured to the end, the importance of this instruction rings clear.

Poet John Milton wrote, "Who best can suffer, best can do."[10] Milton's greatest works were produced during that period of life in which he suffered most, when he was stricken with blindness. Even the loss of physical well-being does not keep courageous men from zealously pursuing their struggle of life.

And so as we honor those who have endured, let us also acknowledge those who are enduring, especially those who carry the heavy burden of broken health.

Illness often moves us into a realm of introspection, of self-analysis. We think soberly about our past and our future — perhaps for the first time. We learn the truth of the statement that it is not ease and comfort that try men and bring out the best in them, so much as trial and difficulty.

Those with lingering illnesses have many hours to spend

alone. But these hours can be used to advantage. As Samuel Smiles once wrote: "It is in solitude that the passion for spiritual perfection best nurses itself. The soul communes with itself in loneliness until its energy often becomes intense."[11]

The soul also communes with God. Certainly belief in God is not meant to provide an escape from the hard realities of life, but it does fortify the spirit of man to face difficulty when it comes. Of course, even the most devout person may occasionally have doubts. But one difference between the believer and the nonbeliever is that the believer soon regains the calm, inner strength so necessary for times of trial.

There is much in life that we cannot comprehend, and though we may not understand the full meaning of the trials through which even the best must pass, we must have faith in the Master's grand design, of which our individual lives form a small part. We must do as he asked. We must have the faith to endure to the end. Surely those who have endured to the end, who have gone ahead, are shouting to us words of encouragement.

The Joy of Tribulation

When we reminisce, we usually remember the happy times. Happiness and the joy we take in living are the promontories from which we are able to appreciate the past and look to the future with hope.

But character and virtue are not shaped and perfected by pleasure alone. And although it may be hard for us in the moment of trial to admit its value, our lives are made whole not only by the *life* we enjoy but also by the *living* we suffer.

The nineteenth-century Scottish cleric Thomas Guthrie observed: "As in nature, and in the arts, so in grace: it is rough treatment that gives souls, as well as stones, their lustre. The more the diamond is cut, the brighter it sparkles; and in what seems hard dealing, God has no end in view but to perfect our graces. He sends tribulations, but tells us their purpose."

The apostle Paul told the Romans that the purpose of tribulations is that "tribulation worketh patience; and patience, experience; and experience, hope." (Romans 5:3–4.)

It is that hope which is most important and which may be most difficult in the moment of our tribulation. So it was for the pioneers who settled the valleys of Utah. Driven from their homes because of their faith, they marked the Mormon Trail to Utah with the graves of their dead. As historian Leonard Arrington remarked of that time, "Of the sixty-two babies delivered by midwife Patty Sessions in the fall and winter of 1846-1847, twenty-two died within a few months of birth."[12]

Even the hymn "Come, Come, Ye Saints," written during the pioneer exodus across the American plains to the Intermountain West, anticipates the possibility of death rather than deliverance. But even in that moment of tribulation is hope:

> And should we die before our journey's through,
> Happy day! All is well!
> We then are free from toil and sorrow, too;
> With the just we shall dwell!

In spite of the hardships — perhaps because of them — that overland crossing has become an emblem of faith and courage that not only established civilization in the wilderness but also has inspired future generations and taught us the meaning and the truth of hope.

As it is with history, so it is with our lives: eventually, the tribulations pass away, leaving us with the goal for which we have suffered, leaving us with the promontories from which we can look back on the valleys and take joy in the distances we have come — and have yet to go. As the hymn also teaches:

> But if our lives are spared again
> To see the Saints their rest obtain,
> Oh, how we'll make this chorus swell —
> All is well! All is well!

On the Edge

In many climates in the northern hemisphere, we are on the edge of spring. It is so close that soon we'll see signs of life: sap rising within the trees; buds pushing through burnished soil; birds returning to build nests. It is a time when all that appears dead blossoms with new life.

How foolish it would be to take appearances of winter as sure evidence that there will be no spring, that all will be eternally dormant. Yet, that is often what we do to ourselves when we encounter life's darker moments. Disappointment, grief, or frustration may bear down on us with such fury that we see it as eternal, as an endless state from which there is no escape.

Perhaps that is why, of all the virtues, none is more needed than unwearying patience and steady endurance. No one is exempt from adversity. No one will pass through this existence without opening his or her doors to an unwelcome guest — heartache.

And life doesn't even offer us the graciousness of presenting our disappointments one at a time. Often they come piled upon each other until we can hardly recover. We seek for respite and find only more pressure. It is at those times that our inner resources are called upon in unparalleled ways.

Robert Louis Stevenson said, "For fourteen years I have not had a day of real health. I have wakened sick and gone to bed weary, yet I have done my work unflinchingly. I have written in bed and out of bed, . . . written in sickness, written torn by coughing, written when my head swam for weakness — and I have done it all for so long that it seems to me I have won my wager and recovered my glove. Yet the battle still goes on. . . . I was made for contest, and the Powers-That-Be have willed that my battlefield shall be the dingy, inglorious one of the bed and the medicine bottle."[13]

The battle does go on, and the truer test of our nature will be what resources of patient endurance we can call upon in those trying hours. Sometimes, when we think we can't take it any more, it is only a matter of lasting five minutes longer. Sometimes it is only a matter of getting a truer, deeper perspective. Trial, however ferocious, is not eternal if endured well.

Despite appearances, winter has just about lost its hold for another season. Months earlier, preparations for new life were already underway beneath the frozen ground. We are on the very edge of spring.

In the winter of our discontent, when disappointments fly like snow flurries, we must remember there will be spring. We may be on the very edge of a brighter day. Now is not the time to give up, for it may be closer than we think.

Overcoming the World

The eminent nineteenth-century historian Henry Adams professed himself to be an atheist. The reason, he said, was that his beloved sister had been seriously injured in a carriage accident. He said she was as fine and faithful a Christian woman as ever lived. She prayed and others prayed that her life would be spared; but, instead, she suffered a painful decline and died. Henry Adams said he could not believe in a God who either did not have the power to stop such suffering and death or had the power but chose not to use it.

Sadly, Adams's line of reasoning is shared by many others. Too often people have lost their faith because they felt the Lord could not or would not answer their justified requests.

We do not know all the reasons why some prayers seem answered in even miraculous fashion and others appear to go unheeded. Part of our confusion in these matters is simply what the Lord told the prophet Isaiah: "My thoughts are not your thoughts, neither are your ways my ways, saith the Lord. For as the heavens are higher than the earth, so are my ways higher than your ways." (Isaiah 55:8–9.)

Oftentimes, the Lord is acting on higher principles than we can understand or accept.

And there is another reason. We sometimes hold the Lord responsible for promises he never made. He has never promised that the way would be easy, painless, and comfortable for the righteous. Indeed, more often just the opposite is the case. The righteous have been imprisoned, persecuted, and sometimes martyred for their faith, while the wicked seemed to prosper. In wars, the casualties are not limited only to the guilty.

Even in natural disasters, which we often call "acts of God," the righteous are not always spared. Earthquakes, hurricanes, storms, and floods sweep away the faithful along with the unfaithful. Disease brings death to believers and unbelievers alike. We need to remember that the Lord has never promised that it would be otherwise.

Why, then, should we call upon God and strive to keep his commandments, if our faith cannot save us from the trials, troubles, and tragedies of the world? Because the Lord has promised us a greater blessing than merely protecting us from pain. His promise is that we can rise above whatever the world might inflict upon us. As Jesus told his disciples: "In the world ye shall have tribulation: But be of good cheer; I have overcome the world." (John 16:33.)

No, God is not heedless of our suffering nor powerless to help us. But he has chosen a higher path of assistance. Instead of removing the obstacles, he often gives us the strength to overcome our trials and to grow within.

My ways are not your ways, he said, for my ways are higher than your ways. The greater promise of eternal joy exceeds any temporary relief from mortal pain.

Doing Without

Time was when doing without was a virtue. "If we didn't have it, we did without," proudly rehearse our grandparents. They talk of the Great Depression, of poverty, of bread lines and blackouts — of doing without.

Back then, the first rule of life was thrift. "Eat it up," "Wear it out," "Make it do" — these were the maxims of survival.

In those days, it didn't occur to people that doing without was a handicap. By today's standards, many people in our immediate history were ill-fed, ill-clothed, ill-housed, and under-educated. And, under a modern philosophy now widely held by some too smart to be wise, these people were doomed to failure.

Fortunately, individuals from America's past saw virtue in their plight. They worked and aspired as if there were more to success than environment; as if discipline and hard work were the paths to prosperity, regardless of one's beginnings; as if the right to fail were as important as the freedom to succeed.

And so our ancestors toiled on, believing that "doing without" was no great handicap; holding on to the outdated idea that a boy, any boy, could aspire to this nation's highest office — even a boy as undernourished as Abraham Lincoln; or that a person with little formal schooling could still succeed in science — a person such as Thomas Alva Edison; or that an individual could do without the benefit of sight and sound and rise to become a master of literature and speech — an individual such as Helen Keller.

It was not "doing without," of course, that made these individuals great, but a rejection of the philosophy that success is dependent upon social, economic, or intellectual advantage.

It never occurred to Abraham Lincoln that the cards were stacked against him, that because others had more money, more education, more status, they had the advantage.

Nor did it enter Edison's mind that it was useless to try because he had no college education; he simply plodded on, night and day, blessing the entire world with his inventions.

Helen Keller had every excuse for self-pity and depression. She saw nothing — but a vision of her own worth as an individual; she heard nothing — except an inner voice that said, "You must never quit trying."

It's true that poverty, cultural deprivation, and ignorance are not generally the stepping stones to success. But, in moderation, there are important benefits from "doing without": benefits such as empathy, self-reliance, and determination.

And so, in our haste to give our children everything, let's not deprive them of one of the greatest gifts — the blessing of sometimes "doing without."

A Time to Share

As the hymn suggests, the goodness and love of Christ never fail, but tragic events in our lives are painful still. Sorrow comes to each of us, in one form or another, for one reason or another.

Sometimes it is personal and individual. Sometimes, like the explosion of the space shuttle, a whole nation, indeed, a whole world, may grieve together.

Great tragedies can never be explained or justified in the mind of mortal man. But now is a time when faith in the assurance and eternal love of God must replace our doubt and concern for the present. It is a time to share our sorrow and try to learn from the sacrifices of others.

Tragedy in any form is never welcome, but, for the strong of character, it can be beneficial. If we examine the lives of some whom we honor, we often find that they experienced personal loss and failure. Washington and Lincoln, whose birthdays we mark in February, are honored not just for their accomplishments but also for their character in the face of tragedy. Theodore Roosevelt said, "Far better it is to dare mighty things . . . even though checkered by failure, than to take rank with those poor spirits who neither enjoy much nor suffer much, because they live in the gray twilight that knows not victory nor defeat."

If we share the victory, then we must also be willing to share the defeat. But there is strength in our sharing. The comfort we give is also the comfort we receive. The prayers we say for others bring peace to our own hearts. The brotherhood we feel gives us added courage to go on.

It is often at such moments of common concern that the brotherhood of man is at its best. Aristotle said, "A common danger unites even the bitterest enemies." If only we could have the same unity, the same sense of urgency in expressing brotherhood in our lives at times when life is not so dramatic but when the results are just as important. We're reminded at times like these that there is a need for the brotherhood of man at all times and all places, and we cannot and should not ignore it.

If we must have tragedy in the world, and we will, let us at least learn from our past. We have bonded together to help the starving in Africa, to dig the buried from under the rubble of Mexico, to pull the ravaged from the avalanches of Colombia. And now we have joined our faith and tears in respect for seven American astronauts who died while the world watched. Perhaps their loss can be our gain if it helps us move one step closer to world unity.

As we meditate and ponder these events, let us unite in our determination to bring peace to the world, even the peace of Christ, whose love we need at times like these.

In Process

The scriptures say, "Men are, that they might have joy." (2 Nephi 2:25.) We are left asking ourselves, If that is truly the intent, why is the earth a place of so much pain? It must groan under the weight of human sorrow. We run sometimes without meaning, and die before we intend. We scramble for bread to fill us and, filled, worry if we will have enough tomorrow. Weeds grow in our grass, disease cripples us, disappointment dashes us; and, through it all, we question if something, somewhere, has gone terribly wrong.

Why would the Lord prescribe for us joy and then allow us so much else, so much that is a far cry away? We can only assume that the pain we sometimes face is part of the process of attaining that joy. Like a great novel, we are, indeed, in process — still unfinished. Perhaps the deepest joy can never come to us where we are, bound by giving misplaced importance to the ultimately unimportant; insecure, our self-worth built upon the sand; impatient, our perspective too intimately linked to the pressures of the here and now. It may be that we are not yet prepared to know and treasure the heights of joy the Lord would have us know.

There is a garden bulb that must be frozen before it can flower. Perhaps the human spirit may be such a bulb.

The pain that is a part of every life can, if endured well, burn off the weaknesses in our soul that would always stop us from experiencing a fullness of joy, weaknesses that make us judge others instead of recognizing our dependence on them, weaknesses that make us tremble with fear instead of having faith in the Lord. As one woman said, suddenly made penniless by a business failure but still faced with the responsibility to support a family, "I'll never be upset by spilling milk again." How can we learn to endure if we never have anything to endure?

Joy is knowing calm in the midst of a tempest.

Joy is depending on the Lord.

Joy is extending our sympathies to all of humanity, putting it all in perspective, and overcoming.

The Lord allows us the difficulties we sometimes face in life, because what he finally hopes is that we can sing him a song without a note of sadness.

The Highs and Lows of Life

Those who enjoy life know and understand that life is a process, not a destination. It's filled with peaks and valleys, highs and lows, good and bad. For some, like the apostle Paul, the struggle is often intense and dramatic. For most of us, the struggle is simply coping with the problems of daily living.

But into all of our lives come moments of difficult challenge. Times of death, divorce, serious illness, loss of a job, failure must be dealt with. Yet, we must also remember that there is enjoyment to be found in each day. Those struggling with the loss of a loved one often live in the future to avoid feeling the pain of the present. The rationale appears to make sense on a short-term basis, but living only for the future, without regard for the present, only prolongs the pain and suffering.

Our stay on earth is brief when measured in eternal terms, and so each day should be well spent. High and low times are as inevitable as the turning of the seasons and the tides. To try to keep them from our door is to shut out life itself. Rather, we should regard them for what they are — opportunities for growth. Only when we lose our perspective, our ability to cope and endure and enjoy the good things that come to us each day, do we fall behind in living. That's when our spirits begin to age.

Life is a process, and we need to stick with it. We're all human beings with the frailties of mortal life. The apostle Paul struggled in many ways. He fought to overcome and improve himself. He was troubled by the personal weaknesses he could not conquer. He had psychological burdens, believing he was the least of Christ's apostles. Yet, he endured and became one of the most powerful and effective teachers of the gospel. Through Paul, we learn that there is no such thing as instant perfection. It is not an overnight process. It, like all of our challenges, is a lifelong endeavor.

Maintaining balance in our lives will help us deal more effectively with life's ups and downs. Attaining a heightened level of spirituality will lift us back to higher elevations. And throughout the process, we must remember that we were meant to have joy. Joy is part of God's great plan and enriches the process of life that we experience each day.

"Dark Is What Brings Out Your Light"

If given our choice, I suppose, we would choose a less fearsome world. We would like a place where weeds did not invade the lawn, nor pain invade the life; where best-laid plans worked out, and ignorance did not ever rule over wisdom. We'd like a world where bodies did not age, cells did not deteriorate, nor muscles tire. We'd like a world where there was enough food to feed the hungry, money to pay the bills, and creature comforts for all.

Yet we all know ours is not such a world. Life is not perfect, and ironically, if it were, we'd miss one of the greatest joys of all — our need for each other. If we were self-sufficient, another's arm would be less welcome. If we weren't subject to fevers, we'd not appreciate the cool hand on the brow. If life met our every need before it were spoken or felt, we'd miss the sweetness of gratitude when someone recognizes our emptiness and fills it.

George Eliot asked, "What do we live for, if not to make life less difficult for each other?"[14] It is in that very act — of making life less difficult — that we find love and find meaning in life.

One family, whose father was out of work, found that the refrigerator was growing empty. The parents despaired of what to feed the children in the coming days. One night, the mother came home to find the refrigerator full, the shelves stocked, and a roast in the oven, all provided by a neighbor.

"How could you know?" the mother asked her friend, swelling with new feelings of being loved and cared for. When her life had been breaking into pieces around her, someone had sensed her needs. The feeling of being loved was a far richer gift than the empty shelves had been a trial.

So, we pick our way through life being helped and helping, linked to one another through bonds of dependency that would have never been forged in a less fearsome place.

Robert Frost looked at a nighttime sky, addressed himself to a star, and wondered why it was the dark that brought out the light. Stars may shine at noon, but we can never see them. It is the darker side of life that yields the light for us, too. If we would drive away life's tears, we would also banish compassion; if we forbid frailty, we forfeit the need for strength; if we demand self-sufficiency, we will never learn to need each other. It is to each other during life's trials that we look as the traveler looks to the North Star for a place to "stay our minds on and be staid."[15]

Developing Inner Strength

Every soul will at some time face a crisis so immense it threatens to overwhelm one. It may be sickness, the silent wearing down of nerve and sinew. It may be poverty, the despair that comes from scant supply. It may be uneasiness in the face of uncontrolled change or sorrow at a loved one's death. It may be a slow panic that the stress that gnaws at our well-being will not go away after this week or this month or this project but is just a condition of existence. It may be the moment when we really know that life is not a blissful happy-ever-after but a place of toil, where self-worth is often in the balance.

Whatever its particulars, the stark realization comes that there is no safe passage here. Though we long for guarantees of safety and happiness, none come. Bad things happen to good people. Best efforts are not always met with best results. We've seen times when the deserving suffer and the undeserving pluck the prize.

So how do we, subject to all of this, navigate the waves? What is that inner strength that allows some to face down their fears and remain courageous while others collapse? Despite the storm, some move forward unparalyzed; some do not descend to anger or despair but stay calm; some resist blaming and bitterness and move ahead, confident in life's final goodness.

How do we, then, develop that inner strength? It may begin with a conscious decision, deciding and praying to have the faith that will put away fear. We move swiftly to steady the ship in the storm instead of lying down on the deck and calling ourselves victims. We begin long before life presents us crises to develop our personal resources, our self-confidence, our problem-solving abilities. We rely on the Lord to feed us daily doses of strength, renewing us with the awareness that two can do anything if one is the Lord. We learn life's most valuable freedom: events may pummel us and thwart us, bruise us and weary us, but finally we can choose how we will respond.

Ultimately, life cannot do us in or even bow our heads without our permission.

The Calm of Christ

Recently, a little girl said to her father, "Daddy, I know the opposite of night."

"What is it?" he obligingly asked.

"Day!" she proudly replied, smiling at her knowledge and accomplishment.

And so a child had noticed that there are opposites in life — contrasts in things about us. Someday she'll probably learn to better understand contrasting emotions, those opposite feelings that carry us from one extreme to another.

We know that the opposite of happiness is sadness, the opposite of joy, grief; and that pleasure finds its opposite in pain, and love, in hate. But all these contrasting emotions may be encompassed or overcome by yet another feeling that is not in opposition to anything. It is the feeling of spiritual calm, a calm for which there is no opposite; there is only the comfort of its presence or the stupor of its absence.

One of the great biblical accounts of such calm — and in the face of tremendous suffering — is the story of Job. Having lost family, friends, fortune, and finally his health, Job nevertheless proclaimed:

"Oh that my words were now written! . . .

"For I know that my redeemer liveth, and that he shall stand at the latter day upon the earth: And though after my skin worms destroy this body, yet in my flesh shall I see God." (Job 19:23, 25–26.)

We know very little about Job. The scriptures tell us that he was a good man. But many good men have been destroyed, their faith in God devastated by circumstances less terrible than those that befell Job. Indeed, even Job wondered at his predicament. But beyond Job's wondering—beyond the incapacity of his own ability to see things in terms of black and white, of opposites—there was an absolute atonement, a resolution of the injustices of life. And he was calm.

So, too, was a prophet in a more modern setting who said, as he anticipated his own death at the hands of assassins, "I am going like a lamb to the slaughter; but I am calm as a summer's morning." (D&C 135:4.)

The calm he spoke of is the calm of Christ, the calm assurance that the grace of the Savior's sacrifice is sufficient to overcome any of life's challenges. Though grief and joy may come, there is peace beyond it all. There is the peace, the calm, of God's eternal love.

The Advantages of Adversity

The Lord will lead us to fertile fields and soft-flowing rivers because we are his children and he loves us. But because he knows our potential better than we ourselves do, he will also allow us to be tried and tested in this world. He will let us struggle to develop strength and to learn empathy for the suffering of others.

It is an immutable law of life that growth comes only as we apply our effort. Physical, mental, social, and spiritual growth all work on the same principle. And this applied effort must have some resistance to push against if growth is to take place. This resistance can come from the trouble, frustrations, and difficulties of the world in which we live.

That is not to say that our trials come from the Lord. We bring most things upon ourselves by bad judgment, miscalculation, shortsightedness, and sin. But it is to say that the challenges we face are part of a plan given to us by a loving God to help us realize our full potential.

The late Senator Hubert Humphrey seemed to understand this principle. Even as he was dying of cancer he wrote, "The biggest mistake people make is giving up. Adversity is an experience, not a final act. Some people," he continued, "look upon any setback as the end. They are always looking for the benediction rather than the invocation."[16] Senator Humphrey spoke with courage and wisdom. Even the benediction of this life is but the invocation of the next.

The apostle Paul was well acquainted with the trials of this world. Yet he wrote, "We glory in tribulations also: knowing that tribulation worketh patience; and patience, experience; and experience, hope." (Romans 5:3–4.)

Our Father in heaven is conscious of our efforts, and he will walk by our side. He will lift up the hands that fall down and strengthen the feeble knees. He will not allow us to be tempted beyond what we can bear. We will never be forced to fail.

But neither will he deny us the opportunities of growth and development that come from struggling through tough and sometimes tortuous terrain in our journey through life. The green and restful pastures are part of his plan, to be sure, but equally vital are the mountains we must scale to better appreciate those pastures.

Fortune

It is a platitude to say that the best things may come from worst circumstances. And like most platitudes, this one is occasionally true. Disease may make us ill, but from that illness may come the immunity that protects us in the future. From what is now a blight may spring our greatest blessing.

In 1666 the Great Fire destroyed the great city of London. Seven-eighths of the city was reduced to ashes; eighty-seven churches were burned, including old St. Paul's. Most who saw the smoldering rubble were so overwhelmed by despair that consideration was given to rebuilding London elsewhere. But while many were defeated by the present, some dreamed of the future. The great architect Dr. Christopher Wren looked beyond the devastation to the opportunity — the opportunity to plan a city that would spring from the ashes of London more magnificent than would have been possible without the fire. The Great Fire had burned the field; Christopher Wren was prepared to plant. And less than a week after the fire was brought under control, he presented to Charles II plans for a new city.

Such accounts of courage and foresight abound in mankind's history, and we may take faith from them and be encouraged by them. But it would be naive and untrue for us to believe that all things are for the best. We never are better for having sinned; and there is tragedy that has no purpose, tragedy that has only the meaning we impose on it. But we, like Christopher Wren, must be willing to impose meaning on life; we must be prepared to remove our lives from the arbitrary definitions of fortune.

The Great Fire was not in itself a blessing to England or her people. Indeed, such a destruction might have defeated a less hearty, less faithful society. And yet, we look around us now, and we see no evidence of that seventeenth-century inferno. In place of those churches destroyed, we see churches rebuilt.

God regrets our losses, reaches out to us in our suffering. And there are times when he will respond to our prayers by overwhelming fortune, by delivering us miraculously as he delivered Shadrach, Meshach, and Abednego from the fiery furnace.

And there are times when the miracle is not in our deliverance but in our bearing of suffering and in what springs from it. There are times when the Great Fire must take its course, when the bitter cup may not be taken from our lips.

But from the difficult times, as from all times, may spring the greater glory and good of God, if we have vision enough to see the new city beyond the old.

40

MOMENTS
OF
PERSPECTIVE

The Long Perspective

The wisdom and glory of the Lord are due in part to his ability to view events from an eternal perspective and judge their consequences by that much more accurate measure. We, of course, do not have this ability to the degree that the Lord does, but we can in a very modest and finite way make use of the divine attribute of perspective. The ability to see things from different perspectives is one characteristic which sets human beings apart from all other creatures, and the extended perspective is one of our most useful vantage points.

The farmer plowing a straight furrow is not usually watching the ground immediately in front of him. He is focusing on a fixed point at the end of his field to get a longer perspective on his work and to keep his rows straight.

The draftsman at his desk or the carpenter at his craft find that the longer the measuring device, the more accurate the calculation.

The best way for an explorer to make his way through trackless country is by pointing to a distant landmark. If he concentrates on the area right at his feet, he will soon be traveling in circles.

When ancient navigators learned to take their bearings from the far perspective of the stars, new worlds opened to them.

But a long perspective is more than a handy tool for guidance and navigation, more than an implement for agriculture or architecture. Applied to our lives, a lengthy perspective can give us valuable direction and wisdom.

Rarely do we make bad decisions from taking too long a

perspective. Usually it is the opposite problem. We don't look far enough ahead to see the implications of our actions, and so we get diverted by immediate needs and desires. We may waste our strength in endless side paths and activities that seem momentarily important but don't contribute to our progress.

They may even add to our difficulties and discomfort. The short-term joy of owning a new possession may lead to the long-term burden of extended debt. The short-term pleasure of idleness and procrastination may only produce long-term frustration and failure as we find ourselves unprepared to face later challenges. Succumbing to the momentary pleasures of our appetites can subject us to long-term health problems, and giving in to the dubious satisfactions of sin can ultimately stop our spiritual growth and development.

On the other hand, once we establish a long-term goal, amazing things can happen to our progress. Our mind can then become an internal guidance system, directing us to our distant goals.

As we align our goals with the eternal perspective of the Lord, we feel the peace and satisfaction of knowing that at no time in the future will we look back in sorrow and wish we had done things differently. We will be content that our thoughts and actions are taking us where we ultimately want to go and that the Lord can and will help us to get there.

"Nearer, My God, to Thee"

As we look around, we see people who measure their lives as failures, as drab, as small — and yet, are they? In that rhythm of light and darkness that is our life, we wonder what has significance, what is the moment that will stay with our souls, cherished in memory, leaving us never quite the same?

How do we measure experience? It is a question that has always challenged humanity, and our answer may be one of the most important we make; for, if it is a faulty standard, we may bring ourselves misery through false choices. But if we can judge wisely, we will have not only peace today but also happiness forever.

Some value most their moments of triumph. Life is successful and meaningful to the degree it fills the hunger for personal conquest. Triumph is all important, and times that do not shine with this glory are dull to them.

Others gauge life's experience by the pleasure it yields. It is the calm lake they like, not one where the tempest is raging. Frustration, obstacles, or problems destroy their well-being. For the pleasure seekers, ill health or personal setbacks destroy life's meaning.

And there are those who value life only to the degree it enhances their self-esteem. They like the days when they are strong and giving, when their worth is measured in how much they control.

All of these have some value in life's aggregate; but, like anything of value, they must be carefully metered.

Life offers more than days of triumph, pleasure, or self-esteem; and, if that is all we value, we shall despair. For life is a collection of all experiences. It is more than a race to see who comes in first or a stage to show off our talents. It is our best chance in all of eternity at school, and all that God sends is intended for our education and growth.

If that were not true, how could we explain the rich variety of experience here? It may be that when we view this life with eternal eyes, we may find our most significant moments, however hard or sad, have been those that brought us nearer to God, those that clarified our dependence on him and our need for one another.

Those most unhappy here are those who expect of life what it was never meant to deliver. Using the right measure for experience may be the key to happy living — a measure with eternal perspective that always brings us "nearer, my God, to thee."

Living for Eternity

There is something incomprehensible, unsettling, almost maddening about this earthly existence. Here we are, surrounded by measureless oceans of space and infinite eons of time, while all about us there are signs that this mortal life is only temporary.

And yet, we continue to make little of it, refusing to consider the evidence, believing that things will always be as they are, that what we think important now will always be important: a man spends every waking hour at his chosen profession to succeed at last and then expire from exhaustion and high blood pressure; a woman focuses on fashion, ever changing her hair, makeup, and clothes in order to keep pace with the latest styles, only to discover that the deceased dress only once; another accumulates wealth and material possessions, then learns that the caravan of death allows no luggage.

The truth is that the worldly hopes men set their hearts upon are of little consequence to the eternities. Harsh words, for us, perhaps, but true words. But the lesson is not one of depression or surrender. The lesson of the eternities is to live to the point, to set priorities in life, making every moment yield its full measure of eternal value, accumulating that which does endure. All other activities are but frivolous props to the grand drama of souls along the ascending stairs of infinite time.

And these are some of the things that endure: the sweet love of husband and wife, authentic love developed over long decades of companionship and mutual service, love that not even death can dissolve; the affection of a mother for her children, unconditional love, without measure, without end; memories of home, of a faithful and dedicated father, of affectionate brothers and sisters, of a close and respectful family; and charity, acts of kindness, acts of sharing, deeds of self-denial for others' sake, offerings of time and substance for the poor and the weak.

Nothing eternal is lost in the divine scheme of the universe. All that charity, all that character, all that love can bind together is forever alive. As one writer penned:

> Choose, then, the better part
> To live now for all eternity —
> Where truth and love embrace
> And time and space
> Are metered by the heart.

The Balanced Life

As wayfaring strangers in this world, we find that life, like an athletic decathlon, requires a balanced effort. We must take part in many events in order to fulfill our potential. If we attempt to set records in any one event, we may fall far short in others. Only by approaching the many aspects of our lives with a sense of balance can we be truly successful.

If we spend too much, we're spendthrifts; but too little makes us stingy, and we're called misers. If we laugh too much, people think we're silly; if we don't laugh, people think we're dull. If we talk too much, we're overbearing; if we say too little, we're thought of as boring. Some of us eat too much; others, not enough. Some may sleep too much; others lack enough rest. Some ignore proper body care and conditioning; others almost worship the physical body.

Balance has application in everything we do. The ambitious executive may sacrifice marriage, family, friends, and church — the things that matter most in the long run — in order to achieve wealth, praise, and power. In this sidetracked condition, a person loses sight of the Savior's counsel, "For what is a man profited, if he shall gain the whole world, and lose his own soul?" (Matthew 16:26.)

The Lord expects us to use wisdom and common sense. He counsels balance and moderation, thoughtfully applying all the truths we know, not emphasizing one at the expense of others.

We need the opportunity to play, and we benefit from hard work, but neither should overshadow our responsibilities to the family and to our spiritual development. Too much excitement at work or at play, like too much of anything, becomes addictive. It creates a situation in which the stimulus needs to be stronger and stronger in order to provide the thrills that have come to be thought of as an essential part of pleasure. Too much excitement undermines health and dulls the palate for every kind of pleasure.

Even in the practice of religion, we can be unbalanced. It's important that we do not concentrate our efforts in only one area while ignoring other equally important commitments.

Prayer, scripture study, sacrifice, Christian service—all compete for portions of our time. The emphasis of one at the expense of another brings us short of the Savior's expectations.

We all struggle with problems and temptations, with excesses and deficiencies, with failures and successes. But, when life is balanced, the problems are less threatening, the temptations less attractive, the failures less painful. The balanced life provides never-ending opportunities for success, happiness, and meaningful satisfaction.

"The Impossible Dream"

In the musical drama *Man of La Mancha*, Don Quixote is both a serious and a comic character. He struggles in a world of fantasy and delusion to achieve virtues that are not deluded but real. And, in the process of his quest, he claims victory over doubt, derision, cynicism, and failed faith. He does it by pursuing "the impossible dream."

It is the paradox of Don Quixote that his world of fantasy is, in its way, more true than the world many of us call real. That might lead us to think the problem with our modern world is that there are too few windmills left standing, too few armored knights of the imagination to challenge and conquer. But we would be wrong in thinking so. The metaphors may have changed, but the challenges and opportunities still exist to steal courage and dignity out of the mundane experience.

We live in an age of communication. Data processing, artificial intelligence, networking, media news coverage, editorial comment—through the various "minisystems" of our communications we have linked ourselves into a "macrosystem," a larger system that has its own language, its own devices, its own view of the world. And that view may sometimes be confusing to us. Because we can now gather so much information so quickly, we have a tendency to accept information as fact, when it might yet be merely a point of view.

It was such "facts" that Don Quixote struggled against, because they were not evidences of the real world. The facts of history are forever being rewritten; the facts of litigation are always arguable; the facts of editorial viewpoint are always preju-diced.

Now, this does not diminish the importance of our com-munications, the good they do, the service they accomplish. Rather, it teaches us to be discerning in our view of what is real; it teaches us a point of view that both depends on communications and is capable of being reasonably suspicious of them.

Even as we speak, there are people, like Don Quixote, still jousting at the windmills of our world, refusing to accept the world as others see it, pushing the boundaries, broadening the horizons, teaching us that the world is not so small as we had believed—the possibilities are greater, the accomplishments more remarkable than we had dreamed.

In this world of possibilities, of faith, we may choose to cling to our technologies—or we may join the prophets and poets to find the truth that is encircled by the spinning arms of the windmills that await our challenge and lead us to our own im-possible dreams.

What a Moment Can Bring

It was a clear morning when the family took the dirt road cutoff that edged along the mountaintop. Visibility allowed the sight of layer after layer of blue mountain ranges. They stopped in a meadow overlooking a green valley five thousand feet below to cook breakfast.

The promise of calm was soon broken, however, as they looked across the valley where dark thunderheads began to gather. A slight breeze became a wind, the blue sky turned black, and rain began to pour on the valley below. The clouds boiled toward them, lightning licking the ridges, and the view disappeared before them. They had just closed the last car door when the rain came. There was nothing to do but sit in the car while the storm worked against them.

In less than an hour, the fury let up. Almost imperceptibly the dark clouds began to lighten—one patch of blue sky, and then another. Soon, light again streamed into the valley, and the storm was gone.

This story reminds us of how quickly things can change, of what a moment can bring, of how life can be grand one moment and dark the next.

Sometimes we're lulled into thinking that nothing ever changes in our world, that one day follows the next with a humdrum sameness. When we are in pain, the trial seems everlasting. The present anguish becomes all there is or ever was.

The same is true for those moments of joy. They expand backward and forward to fill all one's history and future.

But just as the storm clouds came and went with imperceptible beginnings—while the family could see only blue sky or were surrounded by drenching darkness—things are changing in our lives long before we are aware. What we must remember is that life is a variety of experiences; that things do change; that what one moment can bring, another can take away.

That knowledge is comforting reality when we are pained. But it is less comforting during happy times. How can we feel secure with full stomachs if we know that tomorrow the pantry may be empty? How can we rest assured in another's love when we know he may be taken?

The answer is there is one assurance, one guarantee—that is the Lord. Through prosperity or despair, his loving arms surround us. Whatever our condition, whatever our plight, whatever our success, he is there. And his constancy tells us something about ourselves, too. We are of shining, infinite worth. Whether we write a masterpiece and have financial success, or come in last and struggle for our daily bread, we are still his children. Our sense of self should never rest on something outside ourselves that can be as easily taken away as a view in a storm.

Only one thing is more sure than change in this world. It is the constancy and eternal companionship of the Lord.

MOMENTS
OF
LISTENING

Listen

Ours is an age of communication. Telephone wires hum with millions of voices. Satellites soar through the sky, reflecting words and pictures to the waiting radio speakers and television screens. Mailbags bulge with correspondence, and the ceaseless drone of human voices fills the air over every city.

The effective persuader is a powerful person in today's society, and communication is preached as a panacea for many of our problems. So, we are encouraged to improve our abilities to get our point across and to effectively state and support our position.

It is good to be able to articulate our views, but there is another communication skill that is equally valuable and vital to the world's well-being, one that may be lost in the babble of voices begging to be heard. That is the quiet and priceless art of listening.

The listening we are accustomed to today is often a faint shadow of the real thing. Bombarded as we are each day with hundreds of messages, we have learned to turn a semideaf ear to much of what we hear.

Effective listening, of course, is more than just being quiet. Done well it is an active and demanding mental and spiritual labor. To listen well demands our full attention not only to the words but to the inflections, expressions, body movements, the things left unsaid, and any other signals the person may be sending out.

Effective listening requires empathy, the ability to put ourselves in the position of those who are speaking to us, to feel as they feel.

Good listening demands understanding of others, their desires, their hopes, fears, and problems. We are always so quick to judge and so slow to understand.

Real listening would work miracles in this troubled world. If parents listened more to children and children, to parents; if the troubled and forlorn among us could find a sympathetic ear; if nations would stop hollering and threatening and listen to the heartfelt yearnings of each other's people — how different this world might be.

Perhaps in nothing do we need to learn to listen more than in our prayers. We cry unto the Lord, and then we cut off the communication, assuming that the prayer is over. But it may only have just begun. The ancient king of Israel, David, sang out such a prayer. He piled praise on praise and sang unto the Lord until a voice came to his heart and said, "Be still, and know that I am God." (Psalm 46:10.) That is good counsel yet.

Those who listen well will hear this comforting assurance and know that He is always there and always watching over us.

The Lord Also Listens

Listening has always been one of the most important aspects of mankind's communication. Even the Savior made reference to it. "He that hath ears to hear, let him listen." (Matthew 11:15.) And the apostle James counseled us to be "swift to hear, slow to speak." (James 1:19.)

But too often in conversation we find ourselves not really listening, merely waiting for another opportunity to speak. Someone said, "We have one mouth and two ears, use them accordingly."

How often do we say to others, Did I understand you correctly? Is this how you are feeling? Are these the reasons you believe as you do? Such questions asked in a sincere spirit of trying to understand can build trust and appreciation between people. And the same principles applied on an international scale can go a long way toward smoothing the friction between nations.

Effective listening involves more than the ears. William Butler Yeats wrote, "I hear it in the deep heart's core."[17] We need to develop that kind of empathy for each other—consideration and compassion that will allow each of us to share our inner feelings and thereby help us lift each other's burdens.

How fortunate we are when we have a friend to whom we can confide our thoughts. And what a great service we perform for others when we really listen with understanding and love. Unfortunately, such listeners are rare in today's busy world. Because of that, many of us go along day after day feeling misunderstood, unappreciated, and unheard.

But we need not feel alone and isolated, for each of us is free at any time to speak our innermost thoughts and desires in prayer to the one perfect being who can hear and understand our needs. We need not wait for some great crisis to cry unto the Lord. Our everyday affairs are worthy of his consideration. We may not find our prayers answered in the way we expect or according to our timetable, but we are assured unequivocally that no humble prayer will be put on hold. Prayers are heard.

And so, we are counseled to listen—listen to others, listen to the Lord—for we are comforted in knowing that he also listens to us.

Hearing Him

In war as well as in peace we often hear about the suffering Christian as if the object of religion were merely to learn to endure well. Being cast into the fire refines the character, we are told. Pain inclines us to God. These ideas are true as far as they go, but to dwell too long on them misses the point. Many of us on this mortal journey suffer far more than we need. We are choked with fear; we imagine negative events that will never happen; we tremble with occasional feelings of worthlessness, though many of these burdens could be carried away if we would just listen to the Lord.

His voice speaks peace even amidst the jumble of daily events. He calms the troubled waters. He would have us taste and then drink deep from a well of joy. Our Father, who knows us intimately, hears the silent yearnings of our souls and, because he knows the beginning from the end, does not let a single detail escape his notice. If not even a sparrow can fall without his regard, do you think your heart can break without his noticing?

He does not choose for us to suffer. In fact, the very object of suffering is to teach us to end all suffering, move far beyond it in our inclinations and our actions, until it is only a memory. The Lord would have us drink nectar, not vinegar; teach us in sunshine, not in rain. But we prolong our suffering by closing our ears and hearts against his assurances and his direction. And, what's worse, we may even embrace suffering, justifying it as good medicine for the soul.

When our souls are clamoring for relief, sometimes all we need do is go and listen. But listening is not always easy or obvious. When the Lord spoke to Elijah, "a great and strong wind rent the mountains, and brake in pieces . . . ; but the Lord was not in the wind: and after the wind an earthquake; but the Lord was not in the earthquake: and after the earthquake a fire; but the Lord was not in the fire: and after the fire a still small voice." (1 Kings 19:11–12.) And the Lord spoke in a quiet "still small voice."

Once, when He visited another people, His voice was heard again. "They heard a voice as if it came out of heaven; and they cast their eyes round about, for they understood not the voice which they heard; and it was not a harsh voice, neither was it a loud voice; nevertheless, and notwithstanding it being a small voice it did pierce them that did hear to the center." (3 Nephi 11:3.)

Pierced to the center with sweetness and calm — that is what we can be, if we will stop amid the clamor and hear the Lord, if we will just listen to the still, small voice.

Listen to the Coach

One distinguishing feature of our way of life is the increasing number of people who are involved in sports or athletic competition. Most young people now participate in some form of organized sports program. And, of course, spectator sports have become a major focus for the use of leisure time in many of our lives.

There are many positive results that can come from athletic competition. The rewards of disciplined practice, the thrill of pursuing an objective as a team, and the wisdom gained from the inevitable wins and losses are among those benefits.

There is another important lesson that successful athletes must learn. Regardless of athletic prowess or native ability, every individual who has aspirations to succeed in the world of competitive sports must first learn to listen to the coach—to listen to the person who has been there before, to the person whose judgment is born of long seasons of preparation and experience. It is the coach's advice and counsel that must be placed before the noisy urgings of the crowd or even before one's own instincts.

Life, too, demands of us this same lesson. We who participate in this most important contest of living must also learn to heed the voice of the coach: our success and our happiness depend upon it.

And so we turn to the Mentor of life for counsel concerning the rules and strategies for success in this existence. Those who knew Jesus best referred to him as the Good Shepherd. This title was used because of the Savior's wise advice and admonitions. Just as the shepherd would lead his flock to green pastures and sufficient water, so, too, will heeding the words of the Master Teacher lead us to an abundant life.

And yet, many times instead of receiving counsel from the Author of life, we accept advice from those who may know little or nothing about the ways to happiness and eternal life. For in the place of the wise guidelines for successful living that Jesus left us, we many times substitute the unwise persuasions of friends, the urgings of fad or fashion, or the tenuous logic of our own reasoning. And in so doing, we run the risk of losing the rewards of obedience to true principles.

And so, just as the best athletes listen to the coach, may we seek to know and then to follow the Shepherd of mankind.

"Be Still . . ."

A class of noisy German schoolboys were disciplined by their teacher and told to add together all of the numbers from 1 to 100. The boys grabbed their slates and began frantically to scribble numbers, hoping to quickly complete the task. But one boy gazed off into space for some time before he began to write.

His was the only right answer. The teacher asked how he had done it, to which question he replied, "I thought there might be some shortcut, and I found one: 100 plus 1 is 101; 99 plus 2 is 101; 98 plus 3 is 101 and, if I continue the series all the way to 51 plus 50, I have 101 fifty times, which is 5050."[18]

The boy was Karl Friedrich Gauss, who grew up to be the great mathematician of the nineteenth century.

It was not just his genius that solved the problem but his method. He stopped for a moment of quiet thought. Most of us are like the other schoolboys. We leap at tasks, thinking we can be efficient. But too often the end of all our effort is disappointing. On a larger scale, we often find that life doesn't have the meaning we thought it would.

What do we do if we arrive at that place in life when there is too much confusion and too little satisfaction? It's doubtful we'll get much help from modern society. We live in a time when too much comes at us too fast, when we confuse speed with direction, hurry for insight. Everywhere there is noise.

But the Lord has some wisdom for us. "Be still," he says. "Be still and know that I am God." (D&C 101:16.) Strange advice for a time of frantic hubbub, to be still.

But what happens when we are still is that we remove the noise from outside; and then, if we wait long enough, we begin the more important task of removing the noise from the inside — the cacophony in our heads. In that calm, in that quiet, a new voice emerges. It is a deeper wisdom that comes from the Lord. It is a whisper reminding us that we know more than we think — that beneath the welter of emotions, there is understanding of what is important. There is wholeness, silent knowledge, the resonance of reality.

To be still requires discipline. It means, instead of leaping at every day in a frenzy, we choose moments to sit aside from all the others. These moments are time simply to be still, to connect again with the Lord and with ourselves. Then, when we move into the field of action, we move with clarity. Our lives are more centered, and we find greater satisfaction in what life has to offer.

Receiving the Gifts

Every time we see someone blow a dog whistle, we are reminded that the world is alive with sounds we do not hear. There are symphonies of sound beyond our senses. Our spectrum of hearing is limited, for we do not hear sounds too low, too high, too soft—perhaps the most beautiful sounds in the universe.

Our sight, too, is dull. Things blur beyond a limited distance. We lose texture and meaning. The colors of the feathers of a bird on the wing are subdued to a mere brown or gray. Even stars in the sky, which burn with an intensity of brightness, disappear before our sight.

How much we cannot receive through our limited senses. But, even sadder is failing to use the sense we have to receive the great gifts given to us. We might ask the Lord to save our souls from being so stooped by care that we cannot receive the gifts of this earth, the jubilant songs of love, or the chill of the first winter frost. We want hearts wide open to experience the bounties of this life.

We might plead, as did Bartimaeus, when Christ asked him what He could do for him: "Lord, that I might receive my sight." (Mark 10:51.)

The Lord gives many gifts for those who will receive them.

Receive the gift of life, with its stained glass myriad of experience—some pieces bright and colorful, others dismal and dark but necessary to the beauty of the entire picture.

Receive the breadth of his physical creation, where he lavishes us with infinite variety, with not one kind of tree but a thousand, not one kind of rose but flowers of every color.

Receive the intimacy of his caring, a love that penetrates to the level of our most personal need in a universe that, at first glance, appears vast and indifferent.

Receive his challenges for us with trust that the Lord knows what he is doing in our individual lives. What may appear as unendurable suffering may be the very thing that transforms us into a person capable of greater joy.

Those who have most praise for the Lord are those who have fully learned to receive his gifts, who understand the meaning of the gifts of Christmas. If we can trust the Lord enough to throw open our hearts to experience, we will learn that his gifts are good.

Listen to the Heart

There is a traditional Dutch proverb that states simply, "The heart never lies."

Whether we should rely upon the intuition of our inner feelings in every case, as the proverb suggests, is subject for debate. Certainly, intuition must be tempered with reason. A judgment or decision that is made wholly on the basis of one's own internal response, with a total disregard for the evidence or experience, is generally an unwise judgment. But perhaps our reliance on modern technology in all areas of human endeavor has made us too objective, too prone to look outward for decision-making support, rather than inward to the proofs that each person carries as conscience or inspiration.

We now look to computers, recorders, data processors, and a wide assortment of additional information systems to provide us a base for almost every major decision. So, we arrange the diagrams, the computer printouts, the statistical reports, and then we decide which stock to buy, or which market will produce the most yield, or even which automobile we will buy. Thus, like the ostrich, which lost the use of its wings because of its reliance on its legs, we who rely totally upon the faculties of deductive logic may lose the powers of intuition, powers that can extend the faculties of reason and in some cases provide the answers when empirical proofs or experience fail.

Pascal, the French philosopher and mathematician, made this observation about the respective roles of intuition and reason: "The heart has reasons that reason cannot know."[19] Pascal's defense of faith spoken three centuries ago still rings true. For there are yet truths that are inscribed only upon the fleshy tablets of the heart, truths that cannot be proven or disproven with logic or observation.

Indeed, what is faith in God, if not an acceptance of the subtle doctrines of belief that spring from our own internal font of knowledge?

With all of our sophistication and technology, may we still, at times, turn inward and listen patiently to the soft but audible whisperings of the heart.

MOMENTS
OF
LEARNING

To Be Truly Educated

Today we reflect on the meaning of a couplet from the English poet Alexander Pope. The short rhyme talks about the necessity for a complete education and reads like this: "A little learning is a dangerous thing; / Drink deep, or taste not the Pierian spring."[20]

Pope refers here to the mythological fountain of knowledge and wisdom. He suggests that a small drink of learning is not only insufficient but also dangerous, that a little education is worse than none at all. He also advises us to "drink deep" from the well of knowledge, to become more than superficially educated, to become truly educated.

What is that? The truly educated man or woman is one who has schooled the whole person, not only the mind but the heart and the hand as well.

First the mind. Knowledge is mind, and mind is knowledge — and the great mind seeks knowledge in all directions. To truly educate the mind is to expand it widely along as much of the spectrum of knowledge as possible, to make it well-proportioned and balanced. The mathematician, though he or she may be a genius at numbers, is not well schooled without a corresponding foundation in the humanities. And the poet may be gifted in rhyme and meter but cannot be well-versed without an understanding of the physical world of physics, chemistry, and natural science.

And the heart? To train the whole person is to discipline the heart as well as the mind, for feelings guide the mind.

Napoleon was an intellectual without a heart. He was a giant of strategy and logic but a pygmy of affection and human kindness. To discipline the heart is to develop patience, temperance, charity, and to live the Golden Rule.

And then the hand. To be truly educated, one must also train the hand, for wisdom includes the proper and efficient application of knowledge. To think and to feel are authentic earmarks of education, but to do is the sign of true culture. The man or woman who both possesses and applies knowledge—who knows how to lay concrete, to play a violin concerto, to bake an award-winning cherry pie—is genuinely educated.

So, Alexander Pope was right. A little learning *is* a dangerous thing, but true education, which includes educating the mind, the heart, and the hand, is a blessed thing when we drink deep from life's Pierian spring.

False Assumptions

Misinformation is often the cause of ignorance. With little effort on our part, we become victims of, and even pass on, untruths that we assume to be accurate. It would probably amaze us if we knew how many things we believe to be true that, in fact, are not true.

For instance, it seems silly to ask, "Where was the Battle of Bunker Hill fought?" But the apparent, obvious answer is not the right one. The shots heard at that Revolutionary War battle were fired on Breed's Hill, not Bunker Hill. And who said, "Elementary, my dear Watson"? Apparently not Sherlock Holmes. At least not Conan Doyle's Sherlock, because the quotation is not in any of Doyle's stories. And so it is with so many things we believe to be true. We all carry around with us a load of misinformation.

Granted, many such factual miscues, which come from our inadvertent ignorance, probably don't hurt us. But we also carry many false ideas about life and how we ought to proceed in life that are dangerous and damaging. These illogical and irrational ideas slowly and silently convince us.

Many really believe, for example, that we ought to be thoroughly competent in everything we do. We believe that that is part of being an adult. As a result, we're reluctant to admit errors, hate to believe we have vulnerabilities, or, worse, torment ourselves when we're not achieving as we think we should, seeing only the trifling flaws instead of the strengths.

It's irrational for us to believe we'll be competent in everything. The very fact that we've expended effort and time in developing strengths means we've left other skills untended, skills that become our weaknesses.

Another false idea that plagues us is the notion that we should reap approval, even admiration, for most of what we do. We look for nodding heads to tell us we've done well, and if our best effort is ignored, we question the value of what we've done. True, we need recognition, but reality reminds us that it does not always come in direct proportion to our effort. For most of us, our actions, even the best ones, go largely unpraised.

And lastly, it is a falsehood to believe that all of our unhappiness is externally caused, that we are simply victims of circumstances beyond our control. To look at the world around us and complain about what it does to us is of little positive value and leads us to believe we have no control over our own destiny. But we do.

Indeed, the expectations we have about life often become the rules that guide us. And since they do, we ought to step back and examine the validity of these ideas. For nothing has the power to make us more miserable than a false assumption.

Study Is the Best Teacher

The 1980s could be called the decade of social inspection. During this period, we have taken a closer look at the social and governmental services we provide each other. And we have demanded of such services greater efficiency, more productivity, and less cost.

Part of this trend has focused on public education. Here we have begun to suspect that modern education has become too diverse, too fragmented, to accomplish the basic objectives of literacy. Allegations have been made that public education has failed a large portion of our population, that many individuals complete public school still lacking the rudiments of learning — such basic skills as reading and writing.

To what extent these allegations may be true is subject for debate. We know that the system has resulted in the education of millions, but we also know that others have not benefited very much from it.

The call for educational reforms to alleviate diagnosed weaknesses in the system is a good and positive step forward. But perhaps the system is not totally to blame. Part of the guilt for our alleged lack of achievement lies within ourselves. Perhaps, along with educational reforms, we ought to make individual reforms — reforms in the way we perceive learning, reforms in the attitudes we generate in our children about education, reforms in our expectations about what the system can do.

Maybe it is time to readmit this basic fact that education is active, not passive, and that, regardless of the system's efficiency in teaching, the primary responsibility for learning still lies with the student.

Part of the problem might be that we expect to be educated in the same way we expect to be served at an expensive restaurant: we want our prepared meal delivered to our table on a platter by an accommodating waiter; we want it to be palatable and tasty; and, most of all, we want the whole process to be entertaining.

But what is true of dining out is not true of education. Learning requires effort and active study; learning demands self-motivation and struggle; learning is, at times, difficult, frustrating, and unentertaining. Learning has its rewards, but they usually come only after the pain and effort of study.

So, to whatever degree the school system shares in the blame, it should be altered. But this eternal principle of individual learning must never be forgotten: study is still the best teacher.

Of Books and Libraries

With our affluence and abundance, we sometimes forget the value of all we have. We flip a switch, and there is light; we turn a car key, and there is motion. Decades in the development, these miracles are now ours for the asking.

We also may enter a library and choose from among the thousands, even millions, a book — a single book — easy to come by, easy to replace, inexpensive, even cheap. Do we sometimes forget or take for granted the value of our books?

But think on this, you who see only paper and print between the cardboard and glue of a book cover — how great a legacy a book, how great the sacrifice, not of paper only but of thought, of feeling, of life itself: each small collection of thin papers represents a man's, a woman's, life, a life of research, of musing, perhaps of agony.

Each book is a page from the lifelong diary of mankind — from the page that Plato wrote: of the Golden Age of Greek thought; from the page of Shakespeare's prolific pen: of human drama and tragedy; from the page of Einstein's flaming thought: of space and time and stars. And yet another page, from bygone prophets: God's word preserved for us in sacred writ.

No, these are not just books, but living men and women, embalmed forever between the hallowed covers of a book, precious lifeblood of master spirits, given a new life beyond the old to touch us with their living thought.

A well-written book can heal the sick mind, provide food for the spirit, drink for the soul. They are friends to the friendless, counselors to the ignorant, recreation and travel to the homebound, and comfort for the desolate. Books are great levelers of mankind, making the same knowledge and wisdom accessible to all.

And because of the value of books, libraries, then, are not just buildings but sacred shrines, ancestral catacombs, where rest the still-breathing creations of disembodied souls.

A library. Here preserved among the countless shelves, the priceless treasury of human thought. Here we may converse with saints and sages, with the hoary knights and kings of ages past. Here we may sit among the Athenian court to hear the last exquisite speech of Socrates, ride with the armies of Alexander the Great, search for faraway galaxies among the distant reaches of space.

In symbolic humility and gratitude, perhaps we should mentally remove our shoes, we who enter a library—for we walk on hallowed ground.

The Freedom to Learn

Our is the age of freedoms: freedom from want and fear, freedom of religion, of social rights and civil liberties. But unlisted among the basic freedoms outlined in the Constitution is one liberty we must also cherish. It is a subtle freedom, a common but sometimes unexercised freedom, a freedom upon which all other liberties are dependent. It is the freedom to learn, the God-given right to search, to ask questions and expect answers, to study what we want, where and when we want, to read whatever anyone has had the audacity to print, to arrive at our own conclusions after sifting the evidence, to combine experience and intuition. This is the right to learn.

The freedom to learn does not guarantee the acquisition of knowledge, for learning is not a passive liberty but an active pursuit. This freedom is a two-wheeled vehicle. Here, the right is useless without the responsibility. Simply being free is not enough. He or she who would learn must actively follow truth wherever it leads, must exhaust the possibilities, examine the evidence, must make study a lifelong pursuit.

We are fortunate to live at a time when learning is so accessible. Nearly every small town has its library; public education is now a hard-won reality; adult education classes are available to almost everyone; and leisure and affluence have provided time for learning.

Despite all this freedom to learn, despite all these resources, we many times neglect to exercise this fundamental right. Books collect dust in our libraries; adult classes are cancelled for lack of participation; some students work harder at skipping class than at what it would take to learn the subject; and, in our homes, we most often reject challenging study in favor of passive entertainment. One author described us as "amusing ourselves to death."[21]

He who fails to exercise the freedom to learn is at once slave and slaveholder, for he shackles himself. When we stop learning, stop seeking knowledge, stifle our curiosity with excessive amusement, then bondage begins. Gradually, imperceptibly, as youth gives way to middle age and maturity, many of us lose this priceless freedom. Happy in our lethargy, secure in our passive and unchallenging existence, we graze contentedly, enclosed by high fences of ignorance and superstition.

To keep oneself free to learn: that is growth; that is happiness; that is life.

Asking the Right Questions

Often in life we're concerned with giving or getting the right answer. But we must also be cognizant of the right question. While on the road to Damascus, Saul, who later became known as the apostle Paul, was asked by the Lord, "Why persecutest thou me?" That question changed his life and made him ask in turn, "Lord, what wilt thou have me to do?" (Acts 9:4, 6.)

What a mighty change takes place when we begin to ask the right questions.

On the other hand, how much of this world's trouble is caused from asking the wrong questions? Michael Novak, a distinguished teacher and author, commented on repeated studies of poverty. He said, "Trying to answer the question, 'what causes poverty?' is a waste of time. Once you answer a question like that you know how to make poverty. The question to ask . . . is what creates wealth, then use those answers to help the poor."[22] That is a subtle turn of mind but a vital one for the world's future.

It has been said that a problem well defined is half solved. Likewise, a good question contains a portion of the answer already.

Years ago, citizens of a small town gathered to decide how to protect their water supply pipe. The pipe bridged a small gully, and the children loved to balance themselves and walk across it on the way to and from school. This activity would bend and break the pipe. So the stern citizens suggested wrapping it with barbed wire or running a small charge of electricity through it, or at greater expense they could build a large fence to protect it. At length, one kindly older man in the back raised his hand and said, "Why don't we just get a stronger pipe that won't break when the children walk on it?"

As it is with world problems and civic concerns, so it is with us.

How often do we look for a better cure for our illnesses when the real question is how do we give up unhealthy habits?

How often have we searched for ways to change our friends or family when the more pertinent question is how to change ourselves to be a better influence on others?

How often do we pray to the Lord to help us fulfill our desires when our prayer should be as Paul's, "Lord, what wilt thou have me do?"

Certainly we need answers to today's problems, but we can't get those answers until we ask the right questions. Then we can claim the promise of the Lord, "If any of you lack wisdom, let him ask of God, that giveth to all men liberally . . . ; and it shall be given him." (James 1:5.)

The Eternal Challenge

It seems to be an ironic age we live in. We have harnessed the power of the sun, but we cannot clear the rain from the windows of the world. We are learning so much about outer space and so little about inner needs. We have put men on the moon and sent satellites toward the stars, but we have yet to bring peace to our own planet.

Perhaps in our pursuit of peace and justice we should adopt the principles and procedures we use in science. Albert Einstein spent a lifetime studying and pondering the nature of the universe. He distilled his findings into an elegantly simple mathematical statement: "E equals mc^2"; that is, energy equals mass times the velocity of light squared.

A child could learn to recite that equation in a matter of minutes. Yet tucked within that small equation are the principles that have helped unlock the energy of the atom and restructure our understanding of the universe. Einstein's laws of physics have been the basis for many of the spectacular scientific and technological advances of our century.

But it is not by babbling recitations and incantations of "E equals mc^2" that this progress has been made. Scientists, engineers, and technicians have taken the principles embodied in that equation and applied them to the problems they faced. And they have been successful.

In the world of manners and morals, of ethics and values, there are also simply stated but profound principles. They, too, can be easily memorized and endlessly tossed off in conversation, sermons, and preachments. And when they are, they have as little effect on us as repeating "E equals mc^2" has on the material world. But when these principles of human relations are applied in our lives, they change our world more profoundly than even Einstein changed the universe.

The basis of these principles is simply this: "Thou shalt love the Lord thy God with all thy heart, and with all thy soul, and with all thy mind" and "Thou shalt love thy neighbour as thyself." As Jesus said, "On these two commandments hang all the law and the prophets." (Matthew 22:37, 39–40.)

When we begin to understand and apply these principles in the same measure we have used the principles of science, we will begin to solve the most important problems we face: the problems of attaining peace and brotherhood.

The Astronomy Lesson

We look to the night skies and see the summer stars. These heavenly lights have looked upon us from their whirling orbs since the dawn of civilization, seemingly unchanged as they meet their appointed revolutions of days and years, seemingly unaltered while the empires of man rise and fall. The ancients saw them, gave them names and human forms, worshiped them, feared them, and slowly began to understand them.

In the inscrutable wisdom of God, knowledge is not free for the asking. All truth, religious and scientific, represents some person's agonizing toil; and some truths represent the painful labors of entire civilizations. Astronomy is no exception. The truths we take for granted today concerning the universe are the result of centuries of detailed observation and experience. The entire history of astronomy is replete with heroic figures who fought their way through dense jungles of superstition, ignorance, and error in their attempt to uncover truth: the Greek astronomers who postulated the shape of the earth and the distance to the moon, the Egyptian mathematicians who began the geometric computations for cosmic relationships, and later the Italian and German astronomers who added their observations to this slowly developing body of truth. Entire lives were sacrificed to the acquisition of minute facts, all contributing to man's awareness of himself and his vast surroundings.

So we come today to our expanding knowledge that we live on a revolving dot surrounded by endless time and space. This planet, this earthly globe that purposefully whirls through the universe with precision clockwork with other spheres, other stars, other galaxies, is part of an unfathomable expanse. We stand on the edge of this cosmic sea, engulfed by measureless oceans of space, and cast, like children on the beach, our metallic pebbles a few feet from the shore to the moon and Mars, to the closest planets beyond.

With all that we have learned, we have just set sail on our apprentice voyage into the entire universe of truth and knowledge.

Thus through astronomy we also discover human truths. As we turn our giant telescopes toward the stars, we find reflected there an image of ourselves. With piercing clarity, revealed against the handiwork of God, we see our impotence and frailty and our dependence upon the Creator of the heavens and the earth.

Not in agnostic doubt nor atheistic scorn do we observe the stars, but with marvel and reverence — considering, pondering, praising, saying with him who brought them into being: it is good.

A Message for Graduates

There is a time everyone in school anticipates. It is the end — graduation. It is also a time usually referred to as commencement — the beginning. As the young, and some who are not so young, graduate and leave the halls of formal education, they begin to realize that they are, in a sense, freshmen again, that the good life is a series of learning experiences.

If the schools have done their work well, the graduates will have developed habits of mind that will be useful in new situations throughout their lives — curiosity, open-mindedness, objectivity, respect for evidence, and the ability to think critically. The graduates should know by now that learning must be a lifelong endeavor if they wish the rewards of continual self-renewal.

We commend the graduates for their academic achievements and scholastic honors, but we also hope the school years provided an opportunity to develop the person and not just brain power. A broad education should instill flexibility, imagination, and awareness of one's relationship with his surroundings.

Part of the benefit of education is to come in contact with different kinds of people. The development of human relationships helps us know ourselves. Strangely, we can know ourselves only through others, and we can know others only through knowing ourselves.

We hope education has influenced the shape of minds as well as the size. Many times those who use their intelligence with charm and humor and individuality are far more enjoyable to be around than those with simply larger mentalities and little else.

More descriptively put, a four-cylinder mind, properly tuned and expertly driven, can generally run rings around an eight-cylinder mind that is cumbersome and self-satisfied. It's a matter of shape — a kind of grasp, a kind of attitude, a kind of approach to the world and to oneself. So we hope this year's graduate has had opportunities not only to expand the mind in the academic sense but also to improve its contour, to enhance its charm and grace.

And if there is a single message to offer the graduating class, perhaps it is to remember that the truly educated person knows that happiness does not come from self-gratification, ease, comfort, or a state of having achieved one's goals. Happiness involves the pursuit of meaningful goals, goals that relate the individual to a larger context of purposes, goals that call for the full use of one's powers and talents.

Graduation is indeed a commencement. It is a beginning toward the best life has to offer—all of which is founded on learning.

MOMENTS
OF
GROWTH

Developing a Life Plan

Aristotle thought an unplanned life was not very productive, because the individual didn't know what he or she was trying to do — or why; didn't know where he or she was going — or how to get there. Aristotle had a point worthy of consideration: we need to think about the future.

We need a good plan to rid life of all the jumble and confusion. Many of us live from day to day, concentrating on the pleasure of the moment, caring little for the effort that distant goals demand. There's a natural tendency to be self-interested, but most of us don't pursue our own best interests. Instead, we follow illusions, momentary desires, mutually conflicting wants. We're directed by whim rather than purpose, and we seek pleasure rather than perfection. We're influenced too much by the world around us, a world that too often chooses short-term gratification over long-term fulfillment.

We may also find that moral errors are the consequence of shortcuts, attempts to get results in the wrong way. No result of any importance can be achieved in an instant.

The younger we are, the less likely it is that we have a plan for living. When we're young, our goals seem to be immediate ones — things to do, things to get, things to be enjoyed today.

As we grow older and more purposeful, we try to fit our various purposes together into a coherent scheme for living. We learn to plan. We learn we can't do it all at once, and we learn to be flexible in changing conditions to fit our most important goals.

Life offers many opportunities to choose, and every choice we make brings consequences. Not every plan is the right plan; and wrong ones, if adopted, will lead to an unhappy and unfulfilled life. We all want happy consequences, and we all want to succeed. But some forget that success is not a single achievement. There will always be new choices to face and new consequences to consider. Success is always possible, but it's never final. It must constantly be renewed. As a general rule of thumb, things gained quickly can be lost quickly.

Perhaps the great paradox in developing a life plan is that we never really gain control over our own mind and will until we ultimately surrender ourselves to something higher. The beginning of true self-control comes in giving ourselves to others. It is a lesson and a promise that have been taught by the masters for centuries — that only when we lose our lives for others will we find our own happiness and fulfillment. Planning for success in life always involves service to others.

Opportunities for a New Year

This is the time when the year stretches ahead with delicious possibilities, every day yet untouched by grief or shadow or the ashes of broken dreams. In the first of January, anything is still possible. Resolutions may be accomplished, old habits discarded. It is a time to kindle new fires, hope, dream, renew our weariest parts.

The opportunities that will come this year will never be presented in quite the same way again. There is no time like now to cast aside fear and exhaustion and become the person we want to be.

The story is told of the artist Dante Gabriel Rossetti who one day was speaking with an elderly man in his studio. The man brought examples of his paintings and drawings and begged for Rossetti's candid opinion of them. Rossetti shook his head and reluctantly said he could see no value in them whatsoever.

Then the man drew from beneath his coat another set of sketches and spread them out before Rossetti. These, explained the man, were the work of a young student. Rossetti remarked at once that these sketches portrayed a keen and sensitive talent. He was delighted and declared without question that this young student would distinguish himself.

Then the old man said, "I was that student."[23]

What is that gulf that lies between what we may be and what we are? Some say that the problem is in low aim. We underestimate ourselves and settle for less than we could.

Yet, probably for more of us, the reason we don't achieve what we could is a problem of attrition. We wear out. The dream that glows before us like a light upon a hill dims and flickers with time. We are distracted by events around us and cannot focus upon the distant light when we turn back again.

And when our light goes out, we comfort ourselves with faint compensation. We say we've become more realistic, we see things more clearly, we understand our limitations.

Yet, there is a deep stirring within when we see someone who is brave enough to give all. As the poet Florence Ripley Mastin wrote:

> I cannot help but love the knight who goes,
> Unchampioned, derided by his foes
> And friend, to seek the white star of his dream
> In the black night. He only sees the gleam;
> And heeding neither laughter nor the sneers
> Of sane complacency, his course he steers
> Into the starless skies.[24]

With a new year stretching ahead, may we steer a course guided by that gleam, the gleam that leads us to all that is possible.

℞ for Healthful Living

The invigorating activities of springtime seem to be a natural reminder for us to alter and improve our physical actions. The annual renewal of nature that comes in the spring is a catalyst that encourages us to consider improving our own physical fitness.

It encourages us to tailor a program of daily exercise for our own age and circumstance. We need to remember that both mind and body are expressions of life; they are parts of the whole. Bodily vigor becomes mental and moral vigor and is therefore essential to our happiness.

Scientists studying the effect of exercise on the mind have found that it brings significant improvement in learning, memory, morale, speed of recall, and intellectual capacity. It also reduces depression and anxiety.

Physical fitness is the best antidote for fatigue. Repeatedly it has been demonstrated that physical activity at the end of a trying day brings a degree of freshness and renewed energy that nothing else can equal.

For many of us, good health is appreciated only when it slips from our grasp. When it does, we quickly realize its importance, for that personal state of physical and mental well-being makes possible many of the things we enjoy in life.

The body, like any other machine, tends to "rust" with disuse. It needs exercise to keep it running smoothly. It's a fact that a fit person uses 20 percent less energy for any movement than one who is out of shape. The list goes on. Daily exercise helps relieve tension, helps improve sleep, gives us zest for life and courage to tackle problems.

The Lord, too, advocates physical as well as spiritual strength, a healthy body as well as a sound mind. The apostle said, "Know ye not that ye are the temple of God?" (1 Corinthians 3:16.) And we've been admonished to "retire to [our] bed early, that [we] may not be weary; arise early, that [our] bodies and [our] minds may be invigorated." (D&C 88:124.)

Every game has its rules and skills. There are rules for the game of physical well-being as well. If we learn and practice them, they'll give us added years of healthful living.

Self-Mastery

The new year always brings cheerful optimism and a renewed commitment to our personal philosophies of life. It means new beginnings, and it means making resolutions to improve ourselves and our circumstances.

Some of these commitments are broken before we turn the first page of the new calendar. Others are tempered from the initial new year fervor — especially as that fervor relates to the self-discipline of appetites and physical well-being. It's just too easy to settle back into comfortable routines. We're told we need fifty consecutive days of any activity before it becomes a habit. A hundred days is better. Two hundred days assures success.

Of course, many do achieve the goals they set at the beginning of each new year. They improve their lives. Often such individuals determine their course corrections quietly and privately, without fanfare.

The options for improvement are many and varied, limited only by personal vision and resolve. Unfortunately, one of life's greatest paradoxes is that nearly everyone wants to improve his or her circumstances, but hardly anyone wants to improve himself or herself. Self-improvement, increased self-discipline, the establishment of strong values and standards in our lives — all are essential and should be lifelong pursuits.

At the root of all important goals is self-mastery. It has a positive effect on all aspects of our lives. Self-mastery produces a life that is in harmony with individual beliefs and principles — a life that displays congruent and consistent behavior.

Congruent and consistent behavior is the key to happiness and success. That means being yourself at all times, understanding and accepting your own values, and not changing your behavior every time you find yourself in a different environment. If you present different masks for different situations and people, the result is usually inner conflict. Better to display congruent behavior and avoid any disruptive inner harmony, which drains us of emotional energy and blurs our sense of direction and purpose in life.

Living a consistent life — being loyal to ourselves — is the key to success and inner peace as well as to our physical well-being. Living a consistent life begins with self-mastery, and it is a habit worth pursuing as the new year unfolds.

What Is Man?

"What is man that thou art mindful of him?" wrote the Psalmist. "For thou hast made him a little lower than the angels, and hast crowned him with glory and honour." (Psalm 8:5.) David's question, penned many centuries ago, seems equally relevant today. Despite our vast increase in knowledge of medicine, psychology, the world, and the universe, we are still as awestruck over man's potential as was David.

Everything we learn about the human mind and its capacities opens broad new vistas of things yet to be learned. The brain has always been a baffling subject of research and speculation. Ancient philosophers pictured it veiled in mystic secrecy. Scientists of the Industrial Revolution described the brain as a complicated clockwork mechanism or as a living loom, weaving its fabrics of thoughts and feelings.[25]

In our day, the human brain is compared with a computer, but experts are quick to point out that even our most sophisticated computer is little more than clockwork compared to the ability of a person's mind.

The human powers of creativity are incredibly complicated. How is it possible to take twenty-six letters of an alphabet and create a Shakespearean sonnet, twelve musical tones and turn them into Beethoven's Ninth Symphony, or a palette of color into Michelangelo's scenes on the ceiling of the Sistine Chapel?

The depth of empathy and compassion shown in the lives of such people as Mother Teresa in India or Albert Schweitzer in Africa are uniquely human and reflect a spark of divinity in the human character.

The human mind, body, and spirit are the most wondrous creations of God. But perhaps even more intriguing than what we are is the question of what we may become. No work of all God's creations was endowed with such promise as was man. The Bible records, "God created man in his own image." (Genesis 1:27.)

Jesus spoke of our potential for perfection when he encouraged his followers, "Be ye therefore perfect, even as your Father which is in heaven is perfect." (Matthew 5:48.) We are, of course, far from that perfection, but we are apparently capable of infinite improvement. That should give us inspiration for our own lives and respect for each of our brothers and sisters in the great family of God. As we help each other rise to our potential, we will begin to understand the answer to David's profound question, "What is man?"

"Climb Every Mountain"

Perhaps the greatest tragedy of life is stagnation. All else is bearable: poverty can be overcome, ill health can be endured while the mind is strong, and time erases personal hurts and misfortunes. But stagnation destroys beyond repair: it brings meaningful life to an end, makes happiness impossible, ravages thought and intelligence, sabotages creativity.

Nature herself has issued the decree and placed a curse on all inactivity: that pond where motion has ceased becomes a stagnant and salty marsh, devoid of life; that species which fails to adapt and develop with changing conditions is soon extinct.

The same law of progress is applied to human life: where motion ceases, desolation begins. Our mental, physical, and spiritual well-being are dependent upon this very principle. All withers and wastes without growth. Thus, progress is not an extravagance but a necessity, for he who stands still is going backwards.

We have forgotten the very principle of our creation and birth if we have forgotten how to grow. We were born to grow, to reach, to develop continually.

But this is philosophy, and philosophy is less painful than reality. The reality is that each of us chooses to stagnate to some degree. We may remain at our place of employment long after development, learning, and enjoyment have ceased. Words such as *security, tenure,* and *pay scales* keep us there, while words such as *fulfillment, happiness,* and *achievement* slide into our past.

We might obtain a college degree or other mark of educational attainment and then cease formal learning altogether, only to learn that it was not the reaching of the objective that gave us joy but its pursuit.

Ponder life, think on happiness, recall its place in your day-to-day activity — in business, in marriage, in the raising of children, at school — and you will discover that progress and development, challenge and struggle, have been synonymous with happiness.

To be in continual motion: learning, finding, expanding — to watch ourselves grow: minute by minute, day by day, year by year — to pursue one's potential, catching the scent of what we may become — here is the essence of a life well lived.

We can fail at what we strive for, but we must not fail to strive. Once a summit is reached, we must scan the horizon for other lofty heights to conquer, until, as the eons turn to eternity, we have climbed every mountain.

A Parable for Thought

We are all creatures of our God and King, and this is the right time of year to acknowledge it. It's time to give thanks for the good things of life, to resolve to become more worthy recipients, to examine priorities and objectives, to resolve problems and improve personal circumstances.

The Lord has given each of us special strengths and abilities. Many are embryonic, needing to be developed. Some we are not even aware of, because we prefer the familiar activities we know best. But God wants us to seek our hidden talents and use them, lest they wither and die from lack of use.

Recall the Savior's well-known parable, as told in Matthew: "And unto one he gave five talents, to another two, and to another one." He who had five and he who had two doubled their talents, and the Lord said, "Well done, thou good and faithful servant." (Matthew 25:15, 21.) But the one who did nothing with his talent had it taken away.

We must develop our God-given talents. We must explore and try new things. It may be in the pursuit of professional opportunity. Or we may polish our talents in religious endeavors.

Or we may simply exercise our skills for our own enjoyment and fulfillment. But whatever our talents, we must develop them or lose them. A physical skill will become awkward if we don't keep it sharp. If we fail to use any muscle, that muscle will grow flabby. If we never use that foreign language with which we had a brief encounter, we will soon forget even the little we knew. If we read nothing but trivial books and listen to nothing but trivial music, we will lose interest in good books and good music.

And what is true of physical and aesthetic and intellectual talents is also true of spiritual talents such as faith, and love, and friendship. If we fail to listen for and accept the guidance of the Holy Spirit, then we will soon become quite unable to recognize the prompting when it comes. That is what happened to the scribes and pharisees. They had so long refused God's counsel that they were unable to recognize it.

And so, as we set goals for another year, let us remember the parable of the talents and apply that message to our new endeavors. As Tennyson's text for a New Year's anthem suggests, let us:

> Ring out the old; ring in the new.
> Ring, happy bells, across the snow.
> The year is going; let him go.
> Ring out the false; ring in the true.[26]

Developing Our Potential

The potential of each human being is usually greater than the product of our lives. It is generally accepted that most of us go through our lives only partially aware of the full range of our abilities. Why? Well, it may be that we lack the courage to take risks, the courage to risk failure. Successful businessman Ted J. Balestreri once told a group of young scholars that the reason for his success was that he wasn't afraid to fail; in fact, he did fail many times.[27]

A primary virtue of formal education is that it requires us to test ourselves in a variety of activities that may not be of our own choosing—at which time we might fail. Education is a lifelong endeavor; but, when we're on our own, we tend to confine ourselves to the things we do well and to avoid challenges we once failed or never tried.

We also need to free ourselves from the web of social pressure that makes us spend so much time asking ourselves, "What will people say?" or social situations that make us compromise our principles and beliefs because "everybody's doing it."

One of life's paradoxes is that nearly everyone wants to improve his or her circumstances, but hardly anyone wants to improve himself or herself, or at least take the risk to do so. Self-improvement, increased self-discipline, the establishment of strong values and standards in our lives are all essential and should be lifelong pursuits.

In trying to expand our abilities, we should not overlook the spiritual strength and potential that lies within us. A careful nurturing of our spiritual nature will help unfold many dormant talents.

The scriptures tell us of the need to make the Savior and the things of the Spirit our cornerstone in order to deal effectively with the inevitable stresses and trials of life. We are told, "it is upon the rock of our Redeemer, who is Christ, the Son of God, that [we] must build [our] foundation . . . , a foundation whereon if men build they cannot fall." (Helaman 5:12.)

How plain and direct—a guaranteed, risk-free prescription for success. Yet many have "not prosper[ed], but were afflicted and smitten" because of "their boastings in their own strength." (Helaman 4:13.)

Yes, the Lord will help us in all our endeavors, both spiritual and temporal, and he will help us become more aware of the untapped resources within us if we will only call upon his holy name and make him an integral part of our lives.

Resolutions

It is the time of year to put up a new calendar and with it new hope for a new life. It is the time when even under gray skies, things seem fresh and hopeful, and some hidden impulse to new excellence awakens in the soul.

And so we write resolutions and make goals — which we usually discard in a few days. Why? Because when we get right down to the nitty-gritty of everyday living, this year will seem much the same as last. Pressures will grind at us, commitments will chop at our time, and our goals won't be any easier to achieve this year than last. That's not to say they are not possible or won't be done; they just aren't any easier.

Those who really want and expect to do better this year will do well to adopt this operating principle: anything that is worthwhile will be difficult to do. Achievement always has and always will demand a high price. The butterfly who sheds its cocoon struggles, and so must we if we shed our character flaws — or even a few pounds.

It is when we think that the accomplishment of our goals ought to be easy that we give up at the first obstacle. We aren't geared for a battle, and are therefore surprised when we get one.

Forging new habits is not easy because the old ones, like cowpaths in the woods, have been trodden so many times. It is far simpler to follow a course of least resistance than to strain against it and forge a new way. No poem would have been written, no invention devised if their creators had given up at the least sign of difficulty.

Now, this reality should not discourage us but empower us. Anticipating problems gives us the insight and the power to meet them. Paradoxically, once we understand that the battle to master ourselves is difficult, it becomes less so. Then, when things do not fall easily into place, we do not become angry or bitter but tougher. And it is the tough ones who can make their best intentions realities.

For all of us who tremble before our good resolutions this year, wondering if we can ever achieve them, let us be heartened by the words of Lloyd Jones: "The men who try to do something and fail are infinitely better than those who try to do nothing and succeed."[28]

We cannot be improved without first being proved.

A Personal Investment Program

Much has been written about financial investment programs. Stocks and bonds, tax shelters, money markets, and savings accounts have all been extolled as methods of adding to our financial assets and as ways to survive the hardships of economic difficulty.

There is wisdom in this advice. Developing and expanding whatever resources we have not only hedge against potential uncertainty but also adhere to the Christian precept of improvement. The parable of the talents, wherein the scripture praises those individuals who expanded on their assets through wise investment, expresses the divine principle of eternal progression.

In a very real sense, the need for a wise investment program applies as much to the resources of the soul as to material possessions. Indeed, whatever we add to ourselves — to our emotional, physical, intellectual, and spiritual assets — is safer and easier to hold onto than any monetary interest.

True, sometimes an investment in ourselves is more difficult to make than an investment of a financial nature. No doubt we have already broken some of our New Year's resolutions for self-improvement. Many of us wanted to lose weight; others resolved to finish a college degree or vocational training program; some determined to play a musical instrument; others decided to work on Christian attributes such as patience or personal charity.

Regardless of the setbacks or discouragements in our personal investment program, however, this truth is unalterable: that which we invest in ourselves pays eternal dividends, dividends that cannot be stolen, lost, or devalued. And that which we fail to invest in ourselves is wasted, forever lost in the imaginary realm of good intentions and wishful thinking.

Increasing the assets of our character adds to our immortal personality, is inseparable from us, becomes what we are, endures to the infinite reaches of existence. These investments receive interest, have received interest, and shall receive interest in the unshakable order of the universe forever.

MOMENTS
OF
CHANGE

Change and Permanence

Life is a rhythm of change and permanence. Change, because we measure everything in mortal minutes, and time is constantly changing. So much about us seems to be in a state of fluctuation. And then permanence. While much is always changing, we value that which doesn't. Constancy gives us security. We look for it in relationships, in philosophies, in the traditions that bind the past to the future.

Change and permanence. We are made to need and appreciate both, and the earth reflects our need: the waves, changing and unchanging; the seasons, earth yielding to cold and then to warm; change within a constant cycle, a refreshment to our souls.

But too much can be harmful. To exaggerate the pleasures either of change or of permanence in our lives can do us harm. Too much change gives us an appetite for novelty, a need for something in our lives that is never fully satisfied. The very nature of the pursuit guarantees diminishing returns and can bring such tragedies as infidelity in marriage, inconstancy in friendship, or ineffectiveness in completing daily responsibilities.

Those who become addicted to the novelty of change become slaves to the whims of the world. C.S. Lewis said that the Lord wants men to ask very simple questions: Is it righteous? Is it prudent? Is it possible? But if men ask, Is it in accordance with the general movement of our time, or is this the way that history is going? then they will neglect the relevant questions.[29]

On the other hand, those who become too attached to permanence can stagnate, dig deep grooves for themselves beyond which they cannot see. Individually, these are they who take a rigid position and cannot move from it, who are afraid to try new things, who cannot nor dare not risk or try. These are they who considered their progression sufficient years ago and have remained petrified in place ever since. Organizations that dwell on permanence are those that say, "This is the way we've always done it" or "if it isn't broken, don't fix it," not realizing the thing that broke was their ability to change. They fear innovation, quash new ideas, penalize risk takers. Such intransigence, either in companies or individual lives, results in regression, not progression.

Change and permanence. They are two of life's great pleasures and opportunities, but we must always strive to keep them in proper balance.

Adapting

On the world's highest mountains there is a point beyond which no tree can grow. The air is too cool and the growing season too short to sustain a mighty tree. But there is some plant life in the alpine meadows above the tree line: wildflowers especially adapted for the harsh conditions. Instead of being long-stemmed and large like the flowers lower on the mountain, they are tiny and hug the ground for warmth. Their growing season is short, and, perhaps most interesting, some of the flowers face the rising sun in the morning and turn to follow its light all day, until when the sun sets, the flower faces west — a marvelous adaptation to a fierce environment. No longer-stemmed, large flower from the lower reaches could survive above the tree line.

Adaptation seems to be one of nature's great laws, and it ought to be one of ours, too. For while there is the great constant in our lives of eternal laws that must be obeyed, much else about us seems to change. At one time of life we are the child to our parents; at another we are the parent to a child. Our life may bring us days of companionship and love; it may bring us days of loneliness. A sunny day is not a constant, for there is no growth without the rain. Yes, all about us and within us, there is always change.

As an unknown writer suggested, "There is no point at which, having arrived, we can remain."[30] Life is like a river. At no point can we step into it and call it fixed, even if we would like to. A moment may be so precious we would like to clutch it to us and hold it there, but it always passes on.

What are we to do, then, we mortals for whom the landscape so often changes? Like the alpine flowers above the tree line, we must adapt to survive.

Life may not meet our best expectations; our rigid schedules may have to be redone; our tastes based on the quirks of our own personality may have to be widened. Whatever circumstance life may thrust upon us, we must be ready to learn from it and live with it. We cannot call back the past. We cannot lament forever the circumstances that wouldn't conform to our will. When life doesn't meet our brightest hopes, we must simply press forward with courage, willing to give, unwilling ever to give in, always aware that life changes.

From Seedlings to Sunflowers

Despite our best efforts to slow it down, time moves gently on, immutable and unstoppable. The second hand completes its circle, and a minute is gone; with full circle, the minute hand counts out an hour; and the full sweep of the hour hand brings another day to its close. On and on, each sunrise blending quietly into each sunset. Months, years, decades pass swiftly into the past, and into oblivion — so swiftly, in fact, that the present hardly seems real. The present — that fast-moving, evasive butterfly that forever eludes our nets until it is gone, until life itself is gone.

And our children — how fast they grow, how soon the time is gone. From seedlings to sunflowers, almost overnight: the little girl with pigtails bouncing across her back as she races across the lawn in search of dandelions and other priceless treasures is soon the adolescent, in search of other treasures — of boys, of close friends, and, most of all, of self. From there to womanhood is only a moment. And the little boy, with a butch haircut, in muddy, worn-out tennis shoes, is soon the teenager — still chasing, but now it's girls, and cars, and, most of all, life itself. From there to manhood is only an instant.

Childhood. So much to learn, so little time to do it. But time enough, if the present moment is captured, if the day with our children is not allowed to slip away, if we hold as tightly as we can to each second, each minute, each hour with our children.

Yesterday is gone; we cannot call it back. Tomorrow is unborn; we cannot call it into being. It is today that we have. It is only now that we can act. And it is the moment — the present — that counts with children. All can wait but the children. Let the newspaper remain unread, let others spend an extra hour at the office, leave the television off for a while — it all can wait. But the bedtime stories, the romps on the living room floor, the making of doll houses, the Little League games, the piano recitals, the fishing trips, the school plays — these, the precious days of youth that we share with our children and grandchildren, cannot wait. For almost overnight, the seedlings have turned to sunflowers.

The Principle of Progress

With the new year comes also renewed hope — hope that this time we can be better, do better, live better. And, gratefully, one of life's great truths is that we can. We jest about broken resolutions, but the grand purpose for our very existence is change. Inherent in the seed is the flower. Every sunrise means a sunset. Change is a part of every minute of our life, and nothing says we have to do everything the same way we did it last year. Our weaknesses do not have to be perpetual.

But to be renewed, we have to understand the principle of progress. It is faith. If we did not believe the seed would grow, we would never plant it. The violin tune that the child struggles and stumbles over eventually becomes the intricate sonata beautifully played. The runner who is breathless at a mile can finally make it through the final line of a marathon.

It is faith that brings these transformations. Faith in oneself, of course, but of a far more lasting effect is faith in the Lord's love for us. He loves us in a way that may not always be comfortable. His love is something far more stern and splendid than mere kindness. Kindness asks only that its object not suffer. Love demands far more.

As C. S. Lewis said, "We may wish, indeed, that we were of so little account to God that He left us alone to follow our natural impulses — that He would give over trying to train us into something so unlike our natural selves."[31]

But God's love for man is greater than we have for ourselves. It might be analogous to an artist's love for his work. "We are," Lewis said, "in very truth, a Divine work of art, something that God is making, and therefore, something with which He will not be satisfied until it has a certain character."[32]

The Lord loves us so much, then, that he not only asks our change into someone higher and better but will often instigate it for our own benefit. "And if men come unto me," said the Lord in one scripture, "I will show unto them their weakness. . . . if they humble themselves before me, and have faith in me, then will I make weak things become strong unto them." (Ether 12:27.)

So, with enough faith, this can be a year of change. Faith in oneself, of course, to take the first step, to plant the seed. But of more worth is faith in our Heavenly Father, who wants more for us than we could know to want for ourselves.

Life's Impermanence

One of the great themes of literature has always been life's impermanence. Poets and playwrights have looked at the human condition and marveled that everything has its moment and then passes away almost beyond memory. The poet Robert Herrick, who wrote, "Gather ye rosebuds while ye may,"[33] was saying in his own way that the fresh flower of today will be withered tomorrow and dust eventually. And Shakespeare, who was quite taken with impermanence, noted, "Imperious Caesar, dead and turn'd to clay, / Might stop a hole to keep the wind away."[34]

What is Caesar now? In his time he could command armies with the wave of his hand. His slightest inclination became the law of Rome. His coming scattered fear and awe in the hearts of men. But now when we walk the broad plains where his armies fought, we can't even hear the echo of their trumpets. The glory that was ancient Rome is just so many ruins, a pleasant stop for tourists.

Life's impermanence must also strike the visitor to a graveyard. Row after row of markers give us names and dates that barely hint at the passions buried there. Their hopes and struggles for earthly dreams had their time and then faded. Robert Frost looked around him at the first color of spring and said it this way, "Nothing gold can stay."[35]

What are we to make then of this world where each of us struts upon the stage for so few hours? What are we to think of a world where today's hot personality featured in every magazine is forgotten tomorrow? The newspaper that wields power and shapes current opinion will one day print its last issue. Whole civilizations may rise and fall. Where now is ancient Greece, tsarist Russia, Babylonia?

Such contemplations coupled with our own inability to clutch at time, which is forever running past us, ought to teach us two things. First, it is the folly of the shortsighted who put too much faith in things that are impermanent. Power, pomp, wealth, and earthly honor are not true rewards for they bring with them the assurance of their passing. Only the laws of God and his promises are eternal. And second, in a world where nothing gold can stay, we ought to learn to appreciate those things that are patterns for eternity. Relish the love of loved ones. Cherish moments together as if they were our last. Memorize the way our child looks when he turns his cheek just so. Fashion in our mind forever the laughter of our parents for those times when they are gone.

Thinking about the impermanence of mortal life ought not to make us sad. It ought to teach us to treat it as we would all fragile things — with care.

The Value of Change

Change is as inevitable as the turning of the calendar. And with the new year comes the new self. As surely as the tides roll upon the shore, as surely as the seasons redecorate the landscape, we will change. The question is whether the changes will be those we select for ourselves, or those thrust upon us by default and the passage of time.

That is why we make New Year's resolutions: to make certain the changes are positive ones. But forming new habits is like winding string on a ball. One must not drop the ball, lest the good work be undone. The unwinding is sudden; the winding is a slow, steady, gradual process.

Wise individuals understand and seek change slowly and carefully. They set realistic goals, achievable goals. They also work on self-improvement each day, not only at the beginning of the year.

Positive change is not as difficult as it may seem. The secret is to generate more reasons to change than to remain as we are. Then we must exercise the new behavior over and over again as we would exercise a stiff muscle. Soon the new behavior will become a habit, securely rooted in our lives, and the temptation to resort to less desirable behavior will diminish.

We can look to the apostle Paul for inspiration. Paul struggled constantly to improve himself, to overcome his weaknesses, to build upon his strengths. Sometimes he failed, but he never gave up. He never quit trying to improve. He taught us that there is no such thing as instant perfection. He showed us that change is not an overnight process but a lifelong endeavor, marked by occasional setbacks, yet rewarded by the knowledge that we have taken charge of our own lives.

Yes, change is inevitable. It provides a chance for us to grow, to improve ourselves, to improve our families, to improve our marriages. But if we fail to change, if we fail to improve, then we fall behind in living, and our spirits begin to age.

Indeed, if we bar the door to change, we shut out life itself and deny ourselves the opportunity to choose our own goals, to follow our own stars.

When We Can't Wait

The present has an endless feel about it. When it is summer, the sun seems like our natural inheritance, and we can hardly believe that a few months ago we were battling snow. When our children are smaller, running helter-skelter through the house until we long for quiet, we can hardly believe that one day that quiet will be ours. Remember when you thought you'd always be a child in your parents' home? Remember when you thought you'd always be in school?

When today is upon us, it seems like the only reality. But we do have ways of marking off time, the todays disappearing into memory. One season becomes another, and our face suddenly looks older in the mirror. We become the middle and then the older generation at the family reunion. Our parents slip away from us one day, and one of life's anchors is gone.

Though life seems long in the short run, it is but a moment. It flutters past us like a moth, dancing in the light for a second, then darting off into the night. Yet, we should not sorrow but let its brevity make us wise. If time is short, it is precious. If life is fragile, it is to be carefully handled. And in a world where we are taught the importance of patience, we have to understand that there are some things for which we cannot wait.

We cannot wait to mend an argument. What if our harsh words were our last ones?

We cannot wait to hug a child. He'll grow out of the need for hugs while we're busy doing something else.

We cannot wait to treat our parents well. Someday, they'll be beyond our touch, our kind efforts too late.

We cannot wait to give help to a friend. When someone needs help is when he needs it, not some other time when it's more convenient.

We cannot wait to shed our weakness. Tomorrow it will be a habit, and the next day part of character.

We cannot wait to find joy, thinking it will fall upon us when circumstances change. Joy is an attitude, not a future event. Those who wait for it will find they've missed it all.

Our days are like "clouds adrift in the summer sky."[36] We

know their grace one small hour, and then they are gone beyond our reach or comprehension. Let us live them well while they are still upon us.

On Our World

In this universe of unique things, there is not much that is identical. Every pine tree, person, and planet is ultimately unlike every other. But there is one thing that all things in creation share: they are all moving. Nothing in the universe stands still. From the most gigantic galaxy lumbering through space to the tiniest neutron spinning inside an atom, nothing is inert. Everything is active.

If continual motion is common to all creation, the next question we might ask is, "Where is it all going?" Is this movement strictly happenstance and change? Is it controlled by cold, unfeeling laws of physics mechanically going about their business?

From our finite observations, it is impossible to tell where it all is going because our perspective and our field of view are so narrow and limited and our time of observation is so short relative to the vast movements we observe.

But we are not left directionless in our quest for the meaning of motion in all creation. Poets, prophets, inspired scientists, and others through the ages have felt the whisperings of the Spirit and glimpsed a guiding hand behind this constant movement. They have seen direction and destination in its flow.

The destination may go by a number of names. Wagner writes of the "Pilgrim's Chorus" with the strong implication that he means more than just an earthly pilgrimage. Brahms extolls the better land we are bound for in his stirring, "How Lovely Is Thy Dwelling Place."

Yes, the destination may be described differently, but the feeling is always the same — a brighter hope for a better tomorrow, a glorious destination for all humankind and for all of God's creations.

We shall not wander aimlessly in a purposeless universe until light and heat and energy dissipate and all creation dies. Nor shall we go on forever in an eternal circle. Rather we shall progress. We shall go forward, haltingly, yes, stumbling at times, but holding fast to the bright hope that eventually through the grace of God and with his guidance we shall arrive at that fair land that every inspired observer has promised and prophesied.

MOMENTS
OF
GRATITUDE

The Hidden Power of Gratitude

The autumn season with its brilliant colors and bountiful harvests could be also thought of as the season of gratitude. It is a time when our feelings seem to run a little deeper, when our emotions are more vibrant, when the earth gives something back. It is a time to notice the bounties of life, and it intensifies as we approach our most American holiday — Thanksgiving.

Gratitude is a good feeling with a strange kind of healing power. But it slips away, if we don't look deep into ourselves and admit how much we need the power it releases — not just during a day, a month, or a season, but throughout the year.

Gratitude releases a psychodynamic energy. It makes us focus on good and draws us away from evil. This process generates optimism and self-confidence. It also draws our attention toward others and away from destructive self-centeredness. We feel impelled to repay kindness with kindness, favor with favor, trust with trust. Barriers are broken, and horizons pushed back.

Gratitude is a principle that should be pointed out to so-called unhappy people. The best way to counter anger and frustration when things go wrong is to remember all the times when things went right. That is the hidden power, the healing power we sense during the Thanksgiving season. Our challenge is to prolong it.

Perhaps this season of the year, in its own modest way, tries to remind us how much we owe to forces outside ourselves and how much all of us, regardless of status, are in the hands of the Almighty. It is a time to examine our attitudes, to make an effort to refrain from taking everything for granted. It's a good time to look at our own lives. Why were we born at this particular time in the history of the world, surrounded with physical and material blessings?

Many comprehend so dimly the truth of our relationship with God. Many do not know him as the Giver. Many do not understand his gifts, the depth of his love, the wisdom with which he deals with us individually. And so the challenge of the season is to put our feelings of gratitude in perspective. The basis of our thanksgiving should be the knowledge that God has given us all that we have and more than we realize. Throughout the year, we can show gratitude to God not only with prayers of thanks but also by living as closely as we can to the way he would have us live.

The Fount of Every Blessing

Centuries ago Augustine described the simple blessings of his world. He wrote, "How pleasant is the alternation of day and night. How abundant the supply of clothing furnished us by trees and animals. Who can enumerate all the blessings we enjoy?"[37] Who indeed?

Our world has grown more complicated since his time — increased knowledge, medicines to cure our ills, machines to help our work, and other products of man's ingenuity and industry. But one thing has not changed. Our blessings still come from the Lord. He is still the source, the "fount of every blessing." The food we eat, the air we breathe, and other necessities are blessings equally as vital to our souls. Love and work and peace of mind and making progress toward some worthy goal — these are also gifts from God.

The blessings of the Lord have sometimes been described as life-giving water. Isaiah wrote, "The Lord shall guide thee continually, and satisfy thy soul in drought . . . : and thou shalt be like a watered garden." (Isaiah 58:11.) Jesus referred to the words of God as living waters, which, if a man drank, he would never thirst again.

If, then, the Lord is the source of every blessing, and if he is so willing to pour forth blessings as a freely flowing fountain, why then do so many of us go thirsty? Perhaps because we're not prepared to drink. Perhaps we are like hard and crusted soil, which the water doesn't penetrate.

The first settlers to the valleys of Utah found a parched and largely barren desert. There was water, but it coursed in creeks and streams from the mountains to the Great Salt Lake and there evaporated. It did not benefit the land. Not until these pioneers built a vast network of canals, ditches, and finally furrows to lead the moisture to each thirsty seed, not until then did this blessing of water begin to make the desert bloom.

And so it is with us. We must prepare our hearts and minds to feel and recognize the blessings of the Lord. Then we can drink in the moisture of life. Then every sunrise will become a special gift and every new idea an inspiration.

When he leads us "beside the still waters" (Psalm 23:2), we will know how to drink. And having then refreshed our throats, we will lift up our voice in thanks and praise and hallelujah unto him.

Praise God as the Source of Joy

For most people, God is the source of comfort and hope in times of affliction and despair, a balm for the troubled soul. And we are blessed that such a source of divine understanding and empathy exists. He can sustain us through our sorrows. But he can also sustain us through good times. It is human nature to think of the Lord more in times of need than in times when things are going well. There is even a feeling among some that God and the things of eternity are strictly solemn and serious, that smiles, happiness, and joy are things of this world in which the Lord has no part.

But if we see God only as a comfort in our afflictions, we limit his glory and grandeur and divine character. If we exclude him from the good and pleasant experiences of our lives, we limit our understanding of him and his relationship with us. For God is also the source of joy, the source of goodness, the source of beauty. All that is right in the universe is so because of him and his divine plan. As King Solomon exclaimed, "He hath made every thing beautiful in his time." (Ecclesiastes 3:11.)

Through the centuries, writers have tried to convey this message of the goodness of God. Composers and lyricists have created choruses to express their highest feelings of joy and adoration. Painters have dipped into the radiant colors of their palettes to picture the happiness and sunshine of God's good earth and his universe.

Like them, we too can offer our praise and joy for the Lord's creations. It needn't be in some grand verse or chorus. In fact, just a kind deed to someone else is cause enough to feel life's joy. Often the simple is as meaningful as the exquisite.

Certainly, we should use our best gifts, talents, and energies to show our gratitude to God, to include him in things that are good in our lives. If we have the means to create grand monuments that can serve mankind, we should do so. If we are endowed with creative gifts, they should be put to good use in serving others. But even without extraordinary talents, we can have an understanding heart and a humble spirit to reach out and lift others and, in so doing, experience the joy and goodness of life. Any good and worthy work can be a hallowed offering unto his holy name.

And so, all that is really required to partake of God's joy is a sensitive soul. All that is required to give praise and gratitude to him is love for others as well as for self.

Giving Gratitude to God

On one occasion during his ministry, Jesus met ten men afflicted with the dread scourge of leprosy. They approached him, beseeching mercy. Jesus healed them, and they went their way, rejoicing; but one among them stopped, returned to the Master, and gave thanks to him. Jesus responded gently, "Were there not ten cleansed? but where are the nine?" (Luke 17:17.)

We cannot know the thoughts behind the Savior's words;

but given his emotional and spiritual maturity, it is safe to assume that he was not asking for gratitude to boost his own sense of importance or to make others feel indebted to him. Such motives were beneath the stature of the Son of God. Rather, he knew that gratitude is good for those who experience and express it. He had perhaps hoped not only to heal the afflicted lepers' bodies but also to help heal their souls with the balm of gratitude.

Sincere gratitude is perhaps the purest of virtues. Almsgiving can be tinged with self-importance. Being busy, even in good works, can sometimes cause us to be "troubled about many things" (Luke 10:41), as Jesus cautioned his friend Martha. On the other hand, meditations and private devotionals carried to extremes can turn us excessively inward.

But unadulterated gratitude is a pure and virtuous essence. A consciousness bathed in the light of gratitude and thanksgiving sees itself and the rest of the world in authentic terms. In the light of gratitude, there can be no egotistical self-sufficiency. Gratitude gives us a sense of how indebted we are to others. We did not come into this world by our own efforts, and it is likely we shall not be laid away without the aid of others. Our entire life is a litany of those who have lifted us, lent us strength, and guided us along our path. From parents and friends to fellow workers and people we do not even know—the list of those to whom we owe gratitude is far too long to compile.

And if we are indebted to our fellow human beings, how much more indebted are we to him who created us? We can never repay our debt to God. But even if we could, he does not ask for repayment, only for a grateful heart. And he suggests that gratitude is more than just saying thanks. It is best manifest in what we do for others: "Inasmuch as ye have done it unto one of the least of these my brethren," he said, "ye have done it unto me." (Matthew 25:40.) Might we, at this holiday season, give of ourselves in the service of others. And, by so doing, we will show the sincerest form of gratitude and thanksgiving to God.

The Power of Gratitude

The story is told of a person who noticed that his friend was always happy. If there were gray skies, he celebrated the shapes of the clouds; if it stormed, he went out on the front porch to watch and wonder. At each day, he awakened not with anxiety or depression but with rejoicing. Finally, the one friend asked the other, "What is the secret of your happiness? You are not a wealthy man. You are not exempt from the heaviness and pain of this world, yet you are happier than most."

And the happy man answered in one word: "Gratitude."

And so, a lesson for us all: to be grateful for what we have in life. Yet, there are those who will say, "I have nothing for which to be grateful. I am sore and tired. My best dreams have turned to ashes. The world is dark and getting darker."

Maybe. But the very essence of gratitude is learning to love what is instead of endlessly wishing for something different. Gratitude touches the cold stones of reality with light. Are there problems in life? Yes, but we have power to do something about them. That's a reason to be grateful. Is the world sometimes hard and cruel? Of course. But it is also beautiful. Do we cry because life is short? Its brevity adds poignancy to every experience, and we love what we love all the more.

When we are endlessly pining for a different situation, perhaps we should stop and ask ourselves, "Have I seen the gifts I already have? Have I opened my eyes to the heavenly reflections that are already around me?"

God asked us to give thanks, even when there seems to be little for which to be grateful. The reason, perhaps, as in all the Lord gives and asks of us, is for our own happiness. An ancient proverb says, "A gift unacknowledged is a gift unreceived." It is undoubtedly for this reason that the Lord has asked that gratitude be a part of our prayers.

The Savior cleansed ten lepers one day, and all rushed away save one, who came back, fell at the feet of Christ, and gave thanks. "Were there not ten cleansed? but where are the nine?" asked the Savior. (Luke 17:17.) Why did Jesus respond that way? Why did it matter to him? Surely their gratitude could not add anything to Christ's stature. It is because the Lord requests of us only things that add to our happiness.

Gratitude helps give us the proper perspective to be happy. Truly, a thankful heart is a rejoicing one.

The Power of Praise

Two hundred years ago the famous English man of letters, Samuel Johnson, said, "The applause of a single human being is of great consequence."[38] Today it is still true that most of us respond well to a sincere word of praise.

Honest praise and appreciation have been known to affect people's lives for the better; to change a wayward child, inspire quality and cooperation from employees, and reclaim hardened criminals. Praise can lubricate the machinery of human interactions and be an inspiration to the troubled soul.

The prophet Isaiah was specifically commissioned to preach encouraging words to those who mourned, "to give unto them beauty for ashes, the oil of joy for mourning, the garment of praise for the spirit of heaviness." (Isaiah 61:3.) Sincere praise and appreciation can help bring out the best in those who receive it.

But it is not restricted only to those who receive it. What is not so often recognized is the effect praise can have on the person who gives it. Giving praise automatically puts us on the high road of human relations. It is hard to be cutting and critical at the same time we are looking for reasons to credit a person. When we are focusing on the praiseworthy traits of another, our own perspective is raised to a nobler plane. This power to improve is even stronger when we lift our hearts and our voices to praise our Father in heaven. Perhaps that is one reason we have been so constantly admonished to praise the Lord: not that *he* needs it but that *we* do. Sincere and constant praise to our Creator causes us to focus on his divine attributes, to consider and contemplate his godlike qualities of goodness, love, and forgiveness, which we must develop in our own lives if we are to be happy.

King David, ancient Israel's poet and singer of psalms, apparently understood this principle, for he counseled, "Praise ye the Lord. Praise God in his sanctuary: praise him in the firmament of his power.

"Praise him for his mighty acts: praise him according to his excellent greatness. . . . "

"Let everything that hath breath praise the Lord." (Psalm 150:1-2, 6.)

As we praise the Lord, not just in generalities but for specific blessings he has given us, we will find our lives richer and more joyful, our character growing closer to his, and a greater willingness to share our praise with others.

A List of Thanksgiving

As Jesus went about doing good and healing people of their physical as well as spiritual infirmities, he came upon ten men afflicted with leprosy. This horrible scourge of those days was a slow, painful, disfiguring death. Accompanying the physical suffering was often psychological and spiritual torment, because some assumed that the leper had committed sins for which God was wreaking a just retribution. There was no cure. Death, it seemed, was the only hope.

So, when Jesus healed the ten lepers, he saved them from mental and spiritual as well as physical suffering. Surely, this was a day for which they would be eternally grateful. But yet, we are dumbfounded to read that of the ten who were cured, only one remembered and returned to give thanks. It is hard to comprehend such ingratitude.

Or is it? If we look at our own lives, do we see miraculous blessings we've received for which we do not appear to be grateful? It may well be that we have shown God no more gratitude than did the lepers of Samaria.

We who live in America, especially those who were born here, might consider by what providence we are here. In a world where war is often more common than peace, we live in a land that is peaceful and blessed above all other lands. For that alone we should kneel with grateful thanksgiving and acknowledge the source of such blessing.

Many of our blessings are so common that we might fail to recognize them for what they are. A useful exercise in raising our awareness of our blessings is to write a list of them, to consciously enumerate those things of greatest value in our lives.

Such a list might include the names of family, friends, and colleagues. Certainly, our health, physical abilities, and intelligence would be included. Our material blessings should be listed. And what about our freedoms? No list of thanksgiving could be complete without considering freedom.

Having written such a list, the next step is to cross it out and ask, "Where would I be without these blessings?" Now, write the list again. Feel the joy and gratitude as you add each item to your list. Make mental note of those things of greatest value. Try to feel the struggle and turmoil of living life without them.

Certainly, such a list should be the subject of our daily prayers and contemplation. Recalling our blessings in such a way can be a quick and easy way to put our goals and priorities in perspective. Gratitude for what we have gives us humility, motivation, and peace in a world of turmoil.

And offering thanks is not just an act of worship to glorify God. Gratitude and the act of expressing it also make our own lives richer and more meaningful. Perhaps that too belongs on the list as one more reason to give thanks in this season of thanksgiving.

The Red Shawl

In a pioneer diary is this story dated July 1858. The Parker family was traveling west in a handcart company. One night as a thunderstorm blew up, they hastily made camp, and it was then the Parkers discovered their six-year-old boy, Arthur, was missing. Robert and Ann Parker spread the alarm to the rest of the camp, and someone remembered seeing the little boy earlier in the day settling down to rest in a wooded area. He was exhausted from the trip.

For two days the men in the camp searched for the missing child, and then, with no alternative, the company moved west. Robert Parker went back alone to continue the search, but as he left, his wife, Ann, pinned a red shawl around his shoulders. She said if he found the boy dead to use the shawl to bury him, but if he were alive to signal them as he came back to camp.

For three nights Ann and her other children watched, and finally, just as the sun was setting on the next night, they caught a glimpse of the shawl waving in the last rays of day. The pioneer journal records, "Robert Parker came into camp with his little boy that had been lost. Great joy throughout the camp. The mother's joy, I cannot describe." Apparently a nameless woodsman had found the terrified boy and cared for him until his father came. One who later retold the story asked: "How would you, in Ann Parker's place, feel toward the nameless woodsman who had saved your little son? Would there ever be anything that he could desire that you could give him that you wouldn't give?"[39]

To sense what those parents felt is perhaps to get a clearer idea of what the Lord must feel any time we serve and love his children.

We often profess our gratitude to God. We hope in some small way to show our love for all he does for us, and yet we wonder, "What can I do for the Creator of heaven and earth?" The answer is simple. "To worship rightly is to love each other."[40] We divide our flour when another is hungry. We send comfort when he mourns. We lift him when the world would drag him down. And with every gesture, we show we love the Lord.

Proper Appreciation

One day as Jesus Christ roamed into a certain village, ten lepers approached him, begging to be cleansed. Christ told them to pass in front of the priest, and when they did, they were healed. Nine rushed away, jubilant and self-centered, but one returned to the Lord to give thanks. And Jesus said, "Were there not ten cleansed? but where are the nine?" (Luke 17:17.) It was a plaintive question, typical of a lifetime of being used and then forgotten. But though Christ noticed the lepers' lack of appreciation, he did not remove the gift. How many others were healed who hurried off, forgetting the healer? How many beneficiaries of his kindness watched mutely while he was tried and crucified?

"As I have loved you," he said, "love one another." (John 13:34.) And his unceasing service, regardless of proper appreciation, teaches us something about the kind of love he means. Whenever we begin to lessen our acts of kindness and service to others because we do not feel we have been properly appreciated, perhaps it is time to question our motives. Do we do our good acts to be noticed of men? Do we serve for self-aggrandizement? Pats and praises for our gifts to others are sweet, but when we begin to give our gifts merely to receive them, we have lost something sweeter.

There is always the danger that our service may become calculated, our kindness tainted with self. Or worse, if we do not believe we have been rightfully thanked and rewarded, we may cease our service altogether. Hinging our concern for others on their notice of it makes our love as transient as a summer snow. It is the same folly that affects those who stop obeying the Lord's commandments because they failed to see some immediate reward in it.

We may not, in fact, always be appreciated or thanked for the good things we do. That is a reality in every life. But let us not cease to love and serve. Those who can look into a universe that seems almost devoid of the Lord and still pray are those who have faith in him. Those who can serve even one who turns away without a backward glance have really learned to love.

"Were there not ten cleansed? but where are the nine?" And then Christ continued to serve not in stingy spoonfuls, waiting for each thanks, but in feasts where many of those who supped would never thank at all.

Gifts of Praise

There is a hunger in each of us. It is a hunger of the heart, but it is no less real and compelling than hunger of the stomach. It is the need for appreciation and praise. William James said, "We have an innate propensity to get ourselves noticed, and noticed favorably, by our kind." Mark Twain said simply, "I can live for two months on a good compliment."

No one can say how early this hunger shows itself. It may even be that the first cry of a newborn baby is his attempt to call for recognition and attention. And the waves and shouts that every parent is well acquainted with, the calls of "Hey, Mom, watch me," "Dad, look at this," are as important to the proper growth of a child as the food and shelter his parents provide.

We never outgrow this need, though as adults it may manifest itself in different forms, from the healthy accomplishments of high achievers to the sick needs of vandals and psychopaths crying out in their twisted way to be recognized.

Most of us seem to have been born with an ability to enjoy receiving praise, but giving praise may not come quite so naturally. There are a number of good reasons why we may want to develop this trait, however.

First, and perhaps foremost, praising others takes our minds off ourselves. It has been said that a man wrapped up in himself makes a pretty small package. Being aware of others snaps the strings of that small package and allows us to begin to grow.

The second benefit we reap is a healthy habit of looking for the good in others. It is so easy in this often critical world to focus on the negative, and there is always grist for this malicious mill if we care to gather it, but there is also an abundance of good waiting to be gleaned.

The third gift waiting for the praise giver is an opportunity to participate in the finest creations the world has ever produced, because the highest manifestations of man's genius have been done in praise of the Lord and appreciation of our fellowmen. Those whose hearts are tuned to praise find a kindred spirit in these works and a deep "amen" welling up within their souls.

For these and other reasons, then, let us go forth proclaiming the praises of others and in the process bring peace and satisfaction to ourselves as well.

Two Kinds of Gratitude

Someone once said there are two kinds of people: those who divide the world into two kinds of people, and those who don't. This may or may not be true, but it does seem that there are two kinds of most everything. Even such an admirable trait as gratitude apparently comes in both real and artificial flavors.

One form of gratitude is that observed by Frenchman Duc De La Rochefoucauld when he wrote, "In most of mankind gratitude is merely a secret hope for greater favours." This, of course, is not gratitude at all. It is ingratiation — favor-seeking, disguised as thanksgiving. It is usually poured on persons of power or influence and can even work itself into our prayers. It is a glib imitation of gratitude that flows easily from the lips.

True gratitude, on the other hand, is, as Felix Frankfurter said, "one of the least articulate of the emotions, especially when it is deep." It is most eloquently expressed in deeds, not words.

This kind of gratitude is not so concerned with repaying its benefactors as with imitating them in extending blessings to others. It is a "go and do likewise" form of gratitude that creates a chain reaction of goodness as each kindness begets a hundred others.

In the final analysis, this is the most effective form of thanksgiving. We cannot possibly pay back the persons to whom we are indebted: not only our parents who gave us life but the unknown millions of scientists, statesmen, dreamers, and builders who have made our world the place it is.

Certainly we can't repay the Lord. The very breath we draw to give him thanks is borrowed from his earth. But we can fill our hearts with gratitude and then go forth to bless the lives of those about us. Perhaps that is what Cicero, the Roman statesman, meant when he said, "Gratitude is not only the greatest of virtues, but the parent of all the others."

MOMENTS
WITH
FAMILY

Marriage — an Important Decision

When individuals choose a companion for life, when lives and love are committed and vows are given, there is no longer a question of compatibility. It becomes a matter of adaptability and quiet inner assurance that future problems can be worked through and solved. There's no need to look back. In fact, it's a good idea not to look sideways, either, wondering if the marriage should have been to someone else, wondering if it could have been better. Usually, change brings only a different set of challenges.

Recall the Lord's counsel to husbands on marriage and intimacy. He commanded, "Thou shalt love thy wife with all thy heart, and shalt cleave unto her and none else." (D&C 42:22.)

In this brief verse, the Lord commands husbands — and, we add, wives — to do four things:

First, we are commanded to love our spouse, not just to like, not merely to befriend, but to love our spouse in the same spirit and with the same willingness we love our God.

Second, we are commanded to love our partner with all our heart — not 80 percent or even 90 percent but 100 percent. That means to love unconditionally all the time.

Third, we are commanded to *cleave* unto our spouse, to adhere closely to that person in good times and bad.

Fourth, adding much to the other three, the Lord commands us to cleave to *none else* — not to mother, or father, or friends, but only to our spouse.[41]

When there are problems, challenges, or great experiences

to share, who should husband and wife turn to for help, for wisdom, for sharing? To each other, because that is how love grows, strengthens, and reinforces itself.

Good marriages are those where the partners like being together, where they enjoy each other's company, where there is a union of minds as well as of hearts, and where virtue is the strong glue that bonds husband and wife together.

Of course, communication is one of the cornerstones of a solid marriage. Couples should not let things build up inside, should not end the day without having prayed together. It's difficult to pray together if problems have not been discussed and differences resolved.

Marriage may be the most vital of all the decisions we make in life. It may have the most far-reaching effects. That is as it should be, because, as we are told in the scriptures, marriage is ordained of God.

A Mother Builds with Eternal Bricks

Today we speak softly and gently of a mother's love, of sacred recollections, of home, of guidance. We speak this eternal truth: mothers are the fundamental architects of great men and women — not governments, not schools, not churches, but mothers.

There is no substitute. To mothers alone are entrusted the rights and responsibilities of motherhood. She is the one fountain of love that never diminishes. Regardless of our failures, in spite of our weaknesses or doubts, whatever the sin or indiscretion — a mother loves on.

A mother's love cannot be duplicated, not even by father, who shares equally in the responsibilities of parenthood. It cannot be produced in the laboratory nor legislated in Congress. It cannot be marketed in the mass media or purchased at the supermarket. A mother's love is the product of spontaneous combustion. It pours itself upon the forming personality of innocence and writes itself on the timeless pages of each eternal child. A mother builds with eternal bricks — sculpting, molding, fashioning the pliable substance called character.

We cannot — we must not — deprive our children of this irreplaceable affection. It is in being surrounded by the warmth of a mother's love that a child finds a sense of belonging. A mother's presence is the first and most enduring evidence that there is love in the world. These first impressions implanted by mother influence behavior through the course of this life and beyond. For, indeed, to a large extent, we are what our mothers make us.

To be sure, a mother cannot be in the home always, nor would that be wise. To make a slave of mother is to make unjust tyrants of us all. Personal development, recreation, and fulfillment are as much a woman's right as motherhood itself. And, certainly, there are cases where mothers are forced to leave the home to earn enough to live.

Ours is not to judge; but this we state simply: children need a mother's love — not just golden ounces or diamond-studded droplets of it, but bushels and boxes of it, rivers and oceans of it.

Thus, as the centuries turn to eons, when all but character and truth have slipped away, and time and space are measured by the heart — many a loving mother will find that the seeds planted in the obscure dust of daily life have flowered with eternal blossoms.

Our Debt to Dedicated Mothers

We are indebted, this day and every day, to dedicated mothers who love and shape our world. Throughout history, the gentle touch, inspiration, and song of a mother have been a welcome relief from mankind's more harsh and bitter sounds. Her voice has been a vital influence in the ears of a listening child. No force has been more powerful for good than the gentle voice of a mother to her child.

And so, we are indebted; and, as we look to the future, we realize that children — children influenced by a caring mother — are the hope of our world. If the children grow up as people of integrity and character, our future is secure. If they do not, no philosophy or technology will save us.

History has already taught some bitter lessons from those who failed to heed this counsel. We have seen the best thoughts of the human race twisted into doctrines of hatred. We have seen civilization's best technological and scientific breakthroughs perverted and used to destroy rather than to build. We have seen medicines and drugs that could bless and benefit mankind prostituted for money. We have seen the beauties of the earth ravaged for greed. And we have seen the highest ideals of statesmanship corrupted for power.

Why? Because someone failed to remember the lessons of character he learned, or should have learned, at his mother's knee. It is and ever will be the character of the people that defines the quality of life on this earth. And it is mostly in the early years of development that one's character is set. As the twig is bent, so is the tree inclined. When the clay is new and fresh, it can be molded; when it is old and set, it is difficult to change.

How are children and youth best trained to be responsible, mature, contributing adults? There is little question that a good and loving family is the ideal setting for a child to grow, to learn, to be molded; and at the heart of the family is the mother.

It follows, then, that no one serves the community, the nation, or the world better than the caring mothers who caress the babies of the world; the mothers who rock the worried child to sleep, who wipe the fevered brow, who give so much and ask so little.

The world is better served by mothers who develop their own minds and talents that they may better serve and inspire their children, whose hearts provide a haven when there is nowhere else to turn, whose love most closely approximates the love of God for his children.

Every such mother deserves the support and protection of a faithful and loving family — husband and children. She deserves the highest consideration from society; for, without her, society would fall far short. She deserves the praise of poets, the laurels of statesmen, and the humble gratitude of all.

Eventually, it will not be the stentorian speeches, the iron boots, the thundering cannons, or the screaming missiles that will decide the future of the world. No, it will be decided by the gentle hands, the soft caress, the lilting lullaby, the whispered words of love and truth from mothers to their children.

A Mother's Influence

Scholars, poets, and philosophers have long believed that motherhood possesses the greatest potential influence for good or ill in human life. American clergyman Henry Ward Beecher said, "The mother's heart is the child's schoolroom." We know that children unconsciously mold themselves after their parents' manner, speech, and conduct. A mother's habits — good or bad — become a child's pattern for living. Her character is visibly repeated in them.

In many cases, mothers are probably better than fathers in giving advice because they seem to know their children better. They are more likely to know what their children really want rather than what children think they want. The French emperor Napoleon said, "The destiny of the child is always the work of the mother."

One of the most important lessons a mother can teach her children is that they can have almost anything they want, but they can't have everything they want. It applies not only to the things we buy but also to the things we do, to the way we spend our time, to the life-style we set for ourselves.

Every child — every one of us — has to make choices or decisions. And to help make those decisions, we must develop a system of values. The sooner those values are in place, the easier life will be and the more rewarding its consequences. The best way children learn values is by watching parents. We don't have to tell them what is important and what is not. They learn that by observing the decisions we make.

Mothers seem to have the God-given ability to teach their children that most problems can be solved if they think about them, that they can't do anything unless they're willing to try, and that they must accept a few failures along the way. Those are lessons that need to be reinforced over and over again.

Since every child is different and every mother is different, the lessons may take a slightly different form and, perhaps, a slightly different order of importance; but the process is underway wherever there is a loving and caring mother.

Young people don't often understand the full meaning of what they're learning from mothers because, as one writer put it, we never know the love of our parents until we become parents ourselves.

We appreciate the influence of mothers throughout the year. It is an influence that comes in ounces — tiny impressions made upon children hour by hour, day by day, year by year. It reconfirms our belief that the desire to rear children properly, the special ability to love, and the willingness to express it in the development of another human soul make motherhood the noblest responsibility in the world.

What Do We Ask of a Father?

Fathers. Just what do we ask of a father?

He's the one who has to be versatile enough to plow a field, build a house, or lead a corporation; change a diaper, soothe a hurt, or throw a ball. He's asked to be strong enough to protect a family and gentle enough to cry on.

We ask him to love us when we don't deserve it and forgive us when we don't love in return. We need him to watch only us, to see something special that others overlook, even when we're not the star of the team or the lead in the play.

We ask our fathers to provide us a feeling of safety and security in a world they know has none. We ask them to turn a positive face toward us, despite problems of their own, so that we may grow up with confidence.

We expect fathers to teach us about the consequences of our actions, to be firm enough that we believe them and not so strong that we rebel. Fathers have to watch, unflinching, while we suffer the results of our own actions and not rescue us so soon that we do not learn the hard, important lessons.

We hope Dad will inspire us to live beyond our short-term

needs, that he'll help us achieve what we really need and want and not just what we want right now.

We want our fathers to live these things, not just talk about them. One woman, in speaking of her father, said, "I don't remember that he preached order, but many mornings I saw him at his desk, poring over the family budget so we could live within it. He didn't moralize about how we should treat others: I just watched him lift everyone who came into his presence. He didn't command us to be honest, but I knew I could trust his word. He did say, 'When people need help is when they need it, not some other time,' and he lived that way. I know, because I always needed him, and he was always there."

And so are our expectations of fathers. Do we ask too much? Perhaps—just as we ask too much of mothers. Yet, it is the Lord's great wisdom that in this creation we come to earth so vulnerable, so open, so innocent, that we must depend on someone who has journeyed here a few years longer and, in turn, that when we are grown, we have to stretch ourselves to hold another's hand along the way. We are bound to each other in ways we could never be were we not, at one time in our lives, so dependent and, in a later time, so responsible to those who depend on us.

A Sacred Trust

One of the most valued and sacred trusts the Lord has given us is to be guardians of our children. That trust includes the implicit charge of creating a home and family environment that will nurture our children and provide a safe refuge during their formative years.

Today, the home is more important than ever as the place to teach and love our children. And we must do more than just tell our children how to live: we must show them.

If we want our children to live lives of virtue, of self-control, of good report, then we must set the example. If we want to teach faith in God, we must have faith in him. The only way to teach the principle of daily prayer is to pray—together. If we want our children temperate, then we must refrain from intemperance. Indeed, if we want our children to embrace truth and understand it, to be obedient, to love others, then we must cherish those values and act accordingly.

Love is critical to that process. Children need the love of their parents, and they need to love their parents. Love is part of the sacred trust, part of the example, part of the two-way communication. We can show and share our love in many ways. It consists of doing things for and with one another, and it requires the giving of ourselves.

Contrary to those who generate myths about the decline of the American family, a recent national poll—substantiated by family therapists—shows the family unit is not only alive and well but getting stronger. Most parents surveyed said they spend more time with their families than their parents did when they themselves were children. Seven out of ten said their children have more influence on day-to-day decision making than in previous generations. Counselors reaffirm that the family unit is the backbone of an effective society.

Religious orientation is also important in strengthening the family structure. Research over the past forty years shows that religion is related to happiness in marriage and to successful family relationships. And it's more than merely worshiping together. It's also sharing a family life-style, sharing an awareness of a higher power, sharing a common faith and expectation.

Parenthood and the development of strong and cohesive families are sacred obligations. God's love and concern for children, for the sanctity of marriage, and for the importance of the family unit is found throughout the scriptures. If a satisfying, meaningful life is what we want, we would do well to follow the Lord's counsel regarding family responsibilities.

Bless the Hands That Prepare

In talking about a typical mealtime at his boyhood home, author Alex Haley said there was always a blessing on the food. He said his grandfather would add, "And please bless, oh Lord, the hands that prepared this meal."[42] As a four-year-old boy, young Alex said he could never resist opening his eyes just for a moment to look at his grandmother's wrinkled hands. To him, his grandparents were the symbol of all that was noble and good.

Much has changed in the world since those scenes from a small town in the 1930s, but much has not changed as well. It is still true that everyone enters this world because of the willingness of a mother to suffer the labor of birth. It is still true that none of us could survive alone. As tiny, helpless infants, we would soon perish were it not for the loving hands of mothers and fathers.

It is still true that the foundations of all great civilizations are strong families, that mother is a powerful influence in the life of any person.

Abraham Lincoln said, "All that I am and all that I ever hope to be, I owe to my angel mother." His sentiments have been echoed in the words and deeds of men and women throughout the history of humankind.

The Lord commanded us many centuries ago to "honour thy father and thy mother: that thy days may be long upon the land which the Lord thy God giveth thee." (Exodus 20:12.) We owe a debt of gratitude to parents who have selflessly helped us understand that commandment, not for their own sakes but for the good of future generations.

With all the challenges families are facing today, the family unit is still a vital, living influence in our lives. A national magazine polled young college students, asking them who were the women they most admired. There was the expected list of entertainment personalities, sports heroes, notable political and business women of our day; but one group of women got six times as many votes as any other: mothers.[43] These were young people's true heroines.

So long as such love between mothers and children exists, there is hope for the world's future.

Memories of Childhood

The mind is a marvelous thing. Not only does it receive, interpret, and record information daily, but with the passage of time, this wonder sorts and orders human experience. As it does so, it gives increased worth to the memories and recollections of events that seemed less valuable at an earlier age.

As we mature, we begin to understand the nature of human thought and wisdom. And as maturity looks backward through time, it learns that what may have appeared important to us when we were young loses much of that importance as we get older, and, conversely, what we may have taken for granted gains in value as time passes.

"I made a great mistake in my youth," say the words in M.L. Robinson's unpublished diary. "I supposed that what was important to me then would remain important for a lifetime — winning at baseball, buying my first car, dating the high school cheerleader, and making the college fraternity were all matters that seemed of eternal consequence. But age has brought me home to the great lesson we all must learn. As memory takes me back to my childhood — the sports, the cars, the puppy-loves are all gone. And in their place loom the sacred hours I spent with my own mother and father — hours of work, of play, of discipline; irreplaceable hours with parents who are no more."

The truth in those words provides us all with insight. For those of us who are parents, we learn that we do not always have to be understood by our children to be loved by them. And the love we give them, even though it must include a portion of discipline, will be more valued in time. We also come to understand that there is no more important time than that which we spend with our children. To provide children with happy, meaningful memories is a primary responsibility of parenthood.

For the young, this truth supplies a lesson for future reference, something perhaps not fully understood but a precept for consideration. And for those who are now older, this principle confirms our own suspicions, for our recollections of childhood have brought us to the realization of what is of greatest value in life.

How familiar, now, are the hours of childhood to those who are old; and though gone from reality and from present sight, their image is seen clearly through memory's eye.

Something to Take with You

A young boy known for behavior problems was pushed from one foster home to another until one family was found who kept him for several years. With this family he became obedient, responsible, and a good student in school. But at last the day came when even they could keep him no more, and he was to be moved again. On his final day at school, he was rude, destructive, breaking crayons and throwing them, very different from the boy he had become. By the end of the day his teacher was exasperated, and when she saw him out in the schoolyard digging, she ran to confront him. "What are you doing?" she asked, as he hid a small box behind him. Finally he showed her. He was doing no wrong. The box was simply full of soil, earth to take with him from the place he'd been happy. He was carrying away a part of the only real home he had ever known.

We grow up, leaving our childhood homes, and like this boy, we take something with us. It may not be as tangible as a box of dirt, but it is just as real. It is the knowledge that somewhere there are people to whom our smallest triumph or frustration mattered. In a world that is largely indifferent to our cries, once there was a mother who noticed skinned knees and slivers. In a world that passes over our victories, once there was one who rejoiced with us at the first shoe tied, the first speech given. It is inevitable that we pass from the serenity of a childhood home to the disillusionments of the world, but those who have had a loving mother carry with them an island of safety in the soul.

A mother, after all, can make her children feel secure in a life that is dangerous. She can make them feel forgiven in a life eager to bare their faults. She can make them feel confident even when life besets them with problems.

So, though we may not carry them in a box, we do leave home with memories and mementos. We take with us the comfort of parents who gave us a sense of joy even while they knew about world calamities; a mother who believed we were beautiful even though she saw our blemishes; a home that seemed safe even when the wind blew. Across the widening years these gifts to us from family, from mother, continue to nourish, providing inner security where little else can ever be secure.

The Love of Our Children

In Shakespeare's *Merchant of Venice,* Launcelot observes: "It is a wise father that knows his own child."[44]

There is so much in the world and in our lives that can keep us from knowing our children as we should. We are separated from them by age, appetites, style, and perception of the world. An eighteen-month-old toddler sees the world from a low angle — investigating the bottoms of chairs, the undersides of tables — just as teenagers view life from an angle that may confuse and worry their parents.

Each age, each passage in a child's life has its point of view, its revelations, and its blindness. A two-year-old knows nothing of math or science, marketing or sales; but a two-year-old recognizes the pleasure that can be taken in bright and shiny coins, in flowers, in the physical pleasures of a beautiful world. Likewise, a teenager may lack a sense of proportion and may be totally ignorant of the impositions of mortality, but at what other passage in our lives have we known such energy, such enthusiasm, such potential?

Each stage of life awakens in us new capacities and perceptions — which is why each age is intended by God to be cherished, respected, and loved. Paul wrote to the Saints of Colosse: "Fathers, provoke not your children to anger, lest they be discouraged." (Colossians 3:21.) And yet, as parents we are sometimes more certain of our responsibility to discipline and correct our children than of our responsibility to love and congratulate them.

In his essay on parental love, the French philosopher Montaigne wrote that as our children grow and mature, so should our capacity to show our love for them. "It is very often the reverse," he wrote, "and most commonly we feel more excited over the . . . infantile tricks of our children than we do later over their grown-up actions."[45]

One of the responsibilities of parenting is to be certain that our love grows and matures to keep pace with our children's needs. The responsibility of a parent's love is to find pleasure in the challenge of children, to find joy in the maturing association we have with our children as they become adults.

As we sing lullabies to the innocence of childhood, let us also join with our sons and daughters in anticipation of becoming adults. Growing up is like awakening to the many colors and shapes of a kaleidoscope. The pleasure of that awakening should be enjoyed by children and parents together.

A Time of Transition

Early in the second decade of life, young people enter the stage of development known as adolescence. The term itself seems clumsy, and it is indeed an awkward age. But it is such an important time. Unaccustomed physical changes affect the entire being — emotionally, intellectually, and spiritually. The old childhood dependencies are cast aside. For many, it is a time of conflict and confused feelings, a time of troublesome searching. It may take years for the transition to approach stability. But it is also a time of discovery and excitement. What greater discovery could there be than to find oneself? What greater excitement could there be than to explore the value of spiritual and moral commitments?

One thing is sure. The only safe bridge to the new world of adulthood is anchored by thoughtful and understanding adults. Our task is not to provide protection — we cannot protect children from their own growth experiences — but to create an atmosphere in the home that accelerates self-discovery and self-development, an environment where the young person has opportunities to experience himself or herself as a separate individual who feels, who cares, who trusts, who values, and who is valued.

In this kind of family relationship, young people can step forward without fear and then pull back without regret. They begin to know themselves one step at a time. They can test and clarify their values. They can acquire self-esteem and self-regard.

And those feelings, once established, tend to become a way of life.

It sounds so simple, but all parents know the struggle is a painful one. The children who were so close yesterday, suddenly seem so distant, so adolescent. If only they would turn to us for help as they did during those childhood years. But they are searching for help within themselves, struggling for self-identity. And often we are allowed only a stand-by role, ready in case the search goes badly, hoping our own example is a positive one.

Each generation of adults must discover once again, as our parents discovered before us, that our young people are mirrors of ourselves, that they are stronger than ever, that they can resist temptation as we did. They are not turning away from us but are bringing new meaning and vitality to our lives.

They are, without question, our hope for the future.

Going Home

Most of us believe that there was a time somewhere in the past that was far better than today. It was a time when cares were not so heavy or pressures so intense, a time when colors may have been brighter or love more enchanting. It's the idea we have of that summer or of the Fourth of July years ago that today's summer or holiday never seems quite to live up to. The details don't matter, but most of us carry a vision just beyond recollection of a sweeter yesterday.

Now, some scholars say that those almost universal feelings hark back to our own childhood, those sunshine days that trail behind us however old we get. We think of going home and we remember quilts patterned with the history of the family's clothes, the good wool suit, daisies from a cheerful house dress. We remember pies cooling on the windowsill or old trees that were young when Father first watered thirsty roots. Mother's work-worn hands could soothe away the world, and life held a security so warm we didn't know how fragile it was. Going home. A cascade of different images, but always one common denominator. When we were divided and shaken, or when the world dealt us a cruel blow, we could limp home and be made whole.

So home, from our first awareness, has a special meaning for us, and homeless is the saddest term we call another.

It comes as no surprise that going home also means returning to the Lord. That other home, in ways we probably don't yet understand, must have all the heart and passion of the best of this world's homes: a father and mother who sense our slightest need, first awarenesses that burst upon our senses with incomparable joy, and arms outstretched to us. When we are divided and shaken, or when the world has dealt us a cruel blow, we can limp to that other home in prayer, or perhaps in passing from this mortal life, and be made whole.

Scholars may not be entirely right, then, when they say our sense of a lost golden age, the good old days, is merely a shadowed memory of our childhood. It may be a memory of something even before that, of another home and another Father who loves us still.

Home for Christmas

Home. Home is where our mother and our father are. Home is where our children play and think about the holiday season and wonder what bright and beautiful surprises lie ahead. Home is where we long to be and where we need to be, especially at this time of year, when the spirit of the season reminds us that we are members of a family, that we are brothers and sisters, sons and daughters.

Our world is such that we cannot always be home. And there are many during this season who will not be with the ones they love. Our occupations, our educations, and other circumstances of our lives frequently draw us apart, separate us from that home for which we long.

But there is a way home. The birth of Christ promises that way home and not merely in the ultimate sense. Although geography may come between us, our love for one another — which is an emblem of the love of Christ — can make us one.

When Jesus prayed for his disciples shortly before his crucifixion, he said, "Neither pray I for these alone, but for them also which shall believe on me through their word; that they all may be one; as thou, Father, art in me, and I in thee." (John 17:20–21.)

There is no substitute for being home. But just as "home is where the heart is," the heart can take us home, or nearly there. As Christ's love reaches across the time and distance of creation to call us home to our Father, so our love for one another can be a bridge between family members pulling us closer together, no matter how far we are apart.

So in a sense there is a way home to one another and to God. Though we may have wandered far, the joy of Christmas is its promise that the star of Bethlehem is a true beacon and a sure way home. Because of Jesus, because of his birth and his ultimate sacrifice, because of Christmas, no one need wander or wonder; no one is without home or a way to find it.

Homesickness

Of all the sicknesses that afflict us, homesickness is at once the easiest to contract and the most difficult to cure. For we can be exposed to this infirmity with a simple change of scenery or even a temporary move from familiar surroundings. We all remember our first extended leave from home, whether we were at camp, the home of relatives, or away at school — the symptom was always the same: the inexplicable longing for the one place we call home.

Homesickness is common to all people of all lands. As Sir Walter Scott observed:

> *Breathes there the man, with soul so dead,*
> *Who never to himself hath said,*
> *This is my own, my native land?*
> *Whose heart hath ne'er within him burned,*
> *As home his footsteps he hath turned*
> *From wandering on a foreign strand?*[46]

With these words Scott also suggested the remedy for home-sickness. Of all the maladies known to science, homesickness is the only one where the cure and the cause are the same. The only cure for homesickness is home.

The treatment, however, must include more than a return to a specific town, a certain street, a particular house. It must also involve more than a renewed acquaintance with familiar friends or neighbors. The longings and nostalgia we have for home are dependent upon more than people and locations, much more.

A good home is the only spot of all the places under the wide heaven where we are always sure of understanding; it is the one place that will take us in regardless of our failures and mistakes; it is the place where acceptance is not dependent upon wealth or success; the place where we can be happy just being ourselves; it is the place where love is always present.

Yes, the longings to return to this type of home are painful. But it is a pleasant pain, a pain that we happily bear. For even more painful than being unable to return home would be never to have had a home to return to.

Havens of Our Homes

How great is the wisdom of God and the beauty of his creation. But as we look at the world around us and see what man has done to it, we are tempted to believe that we can do nothing to change it, nothing to stop the violence, the pornography, the hate, the tragedy that from time to time bathes our small planet in the blood of world conflict.

Perhaps our best chance at changing the world lies in changing our own small world, in making havens of our homes, creating islands of peace and harmony, islands where love rules.

Making a haven of our home is not to isolate ourselves from the world, for all in the world is not bad, but to provide some guidance and protection. It consists not in isolation but in insulation, in providing a barrier for our family against chaos and indecency. It is an admission that we, as parents, cannot do everything but that we can do something; and whatever we can do, we should do.

This is not an easy task, this making havens of our homes. Our doors are open; our walls are thin. Minute by minute, day by day the intrusions multiply, the unwanted influences increase. But surrender is not the answer, nor defeat the outcome.

We who call ourselves fathers or mothers must place ourselves in charge. We have not only the responsibilities of parenthood but also the rights—the right to decide what goes on in our household, what is watched on television, which videos are viewed, what language is spoken, what books are read.

We cannot, we must not, be bullied by the world. Let those who would live differently do so at their own expense, not ours. Let society preach what it wants. But we, we are in charge of our own.

Permissiveness, dishonesty, obscenity, selfishness, the impure, and hatred—these are the enemies of happiness and shall be kept outside our walls.

Trust, discipline, refinement, humility, virtue, and love—these are the allies of happiness and should be harbored within. They are the values that make this country rich.

Like the ancient castles and fortresses of medieval times with their moats and drawbridges, their towering walls and armaments—all to provide safety from wild beasts and human intruders—we, too, can provide a place of refuge for our families in making homes of our houses and havens of our homes.

MOMENTS
WITH
FRIENDS

Gratitude for Friends

It seems woefully inadequate to set aside only one day out of the entire year for Thanksgiving. We are all recipients of countless blessings, enough to merit the designation of every day as a day of gratitude. The mere fact that we exist in a world of exquisite beauty, a world inhabited by others with whom to share our awareness, is sufficient to evoke continuous and sincere appreciation.

Perhaps not enough has been said of these others with whom we share this world, these friends, these of close association — relatives, husbands, wives, acquaintances.

The word *friend* has several synonyms: comrade, chum, confidant, companion. A friend is one with whom we are safe. A friend has seen beyond the shallow facade of our protective mask to the depths of our griefs and fears, to the heights of our joys and ambitions — and loves us still.

To accumulate wealth is noteworthy; to succeed at business is something; but he who has a friend has done extremely well for himself. With this achievement he has doubled his joy while dividing his sorrow. He who has a friend has at once gained both fame and honor.

It was the illustrious Napoleon who claimed that he neither made nor needed friends. It was this same victorious monarch who spent the last years of his life in miserable solitude as a friendless outcast, alone with his arrogance and greed. He had conquered much of the civilized world but died without a single friend to mourn his passing. On the other hand, when asked to divulge the secret of his long and beautiful life, Charles Kingsley replied, "I had a friend."

In truth, even one good friend can tilt the scales of life toward happiness, regardless of whatever other acquisitions we may or may not have gained. When we are insecure or afraid, we cannot turn to wealth for comfort. It is not fame who will visit us in our maturity to discuss politics and grandchildren. Our possessions will feel no loss at our demise, but our friends will.

May we understand the value of a friend by making friends and by being a friend. Let us keep in constant repair those friendships we now enjoy. And at this Thanksgiving season, let us express gratitude for those who bear the noble name of friend.

Prudent Friendships

Our friendship with others is one of life's more meaningful and comforting supports. The Greek poet Euripides said, "Life has no blessing like a prudent friend." But how prudent are we in our relationships with our friends?

Interpersonal relationships are more important to us than most of us realize. When adults are asked to identify times when they are happy, most indicate that what make them most happy — or most sad — are personal relationships with others. Those relationships are usually more important than personal health, more important than employment, more important than money and material things.

We all need durable relationships in our lives. There is value in an intimate friendship, even though we may risk being hurt by making ourselves vulnerable. Close friendships make us feel wanted and needed. They also help us discover that our own problems and feelings are not unique. Friends often have similar problems — and joys — to share.

Our lives are enriched through meaningful friendships. Perhaps more than any other single factor, the quality of our human ties determines the quality of our lives. So a high priority should be the building of relationships with our family and friends through open and honest communication.

When we run short on friendship, it might be because we are not willing to devote our energies to it. We simply assume it will happen. But it doesn't. We must take an interest in other people, and that requires time, effort, and concern.

Often, we tend to be guarded about what we share. We stick close to role-defined behavior or focus on our positive attributes in order to avoid rejection. But if a relationship is to develop, we have to take the risk of being honest about our feelings.

Sometimes relationships are difficult because they're inconvenient. We may want strong relationships with others, but we find it inconvenient to invest in them.

A recent study indicates that concern for others is a prescription for reducing the stresses of life. Researchers say involvement with others and concern for their problems work wonders. On the other hand, if we're self-centered, we experience more anxiety, more depression, more hostility, and more stress.

Perhaps the simplest, yet most effective, advice ever given regarding our relationships with others came from the Savior's Sermon on the Mount. He said simply and directly, "Whatsoever ye would that men should do to you, do ye even so to them." (Matthew 7:12.) That admonition is the epitome of prudent friendship.

The Gift of Christlike Friends

What greater gift dost thou bestow,
What greater goodness can we know
Than Christlike friends, whose gentle ways
Strengthen our faith, enrich our days.[47]

What more could we ask of a friend than to be Christlike, or more importantly, what more could we give?

The friendship we share with others makes an important contribution to the quality of our lives. We place high value on these relationships, for having good friends with whom we feel comfortable gives us a sense of honesty, a sense of trust, a sense of success.

Friendship is an intangible thing. It is not unlike an invisible force that we send out to encircle others and that, in turn, comes back to encircle us as well. Honest friendship is a circle of power that envelops us in our entirety—all our good points along with all our bad. It is a power that surpasses judgment. It is a bond that reaches not from person to person but from soul to soul.

In order for us to be a Christlike friend, we must adopt Christlike attributes. The Savior said, "He that followeth me shall not walk in darkness, but shall have the light of life." (John 8:12.) Part of that light comes from our relationship with our fellowman: "Thou shalt love thy neighbour as thyself." (Leviticus 19:18.)

If we would be friends, or if we would have friends, we should do as the Savior did. We should be willing to serve others even when it's inconvenient. We should listen with our hearts as well as our ears. We should give our love as freely as we give our advice.

Friendship is a power that lights our lives. It is a gift to be cherished, a part of our eternal progress, a stone in the foundation of our lives. An ancient prophet said, "It is upon the rock of our Redeemer, who is Christ, the Son of God, that [we] must build [our] foundation . . . , a foundation whereon if men build they cannot fall." (Helaman 5:12.)

That is true in our relationships with others as well as with ourselves. Friendship is built upon the foundation of the gospel of Christ, the center of which is love. If the foundation is love, then the building blocks are acts of service. The resulting structure is a strong, lasting lighthouse of friendship.

> *What greater gift dost thou bestow,*
> *What greater goodness can we know*
> *Than Christlike friends, whose gentle ways*
> *Strengthen our faith, enrich our days.*

Laurels for the Living

At first thought, Christ's injunction to "let the dead bury their dead," seems somewhat harsh. (Matthew 8:22.) It may appear especially insensitive at this time of year as Memorial Day bids us to remember departed relatives and friends. It was not disrespect for the dead but respect for the living, however, that prompted the Savior's words—respect for the simple truth of life that service rendered is of little value to those we love if they are dead. Postmortem love, kindness shown to those now absent, is like the rain of September that arrives too late to save the withered crops from the drought of summer.

The love we offer to the dead—the eulogies, the wreaths, the epitaphs—does little to bless their lives. We remember them—as well we should—and remember with great fondness. But how much sweeter would be the memory if we had shared those thoughts more while yet they lived. We often withhold our encouragement and affection from the living, waiting for the right moment to express our love—waiting, procrastinating, busying ourselves with the irrelevancies of life—until at last the moment is gone. The flower bouquet we had thought to carry to a friend must now be delivered as a wreath; the appreciation that might have comforted the aging parent or spouse will become part of the funeral eulogy; the undelivered expressions of love that could have been given to those we knew must now become the epitaphs on grave markers.

George William Childs kept these words as a creed to live by: "Do not keep the alabaster boxes of your love and tenderness sealed up until your friends are dead. Fill their lives with sweetness. Speak approving, cheering words while their ears can hear them, and while their hearts can be thrilled and made happier by them."

Let us remember to love the living while there is time. Perhaps someone waits in a nursing home for a visit that we have been putting off. We may owe some unpaid debt of kindness to a friend, a former teacher, a sister or brother, a parent—a debt that may remain unpaid unless we act now.

Soon the loveliest and the best that we have known will be beyond our reach, and buried with them will be the opportunity to bless them with our love.

Let our eulogies be written upon the fleshy chambers of living hearts. Let our wreaths be gentle words and caresses placed about the necks of those who can still appreciate their fragrance.

It is for the dead to bury the dead—but it is for the living to love the living.

The Circle of Friendship

The most important task imposed by religion has always been to "love thy neighbor" and that includes "love thy family." It is a charge to all mankind to be concerned about the business of human relationships. It includes developing friendships with people we feel comfortable around, those with whom we share mutual honesty and trust.

Being a friend can range from being a casual acquaintance to being someone who hears another's deepest secrets. The relationship differs from person to person, but the bond is always there.

Why does there seem to be a shortage of friendship? One reason may be that so many are not willing to devote their energies to it. Friendship does not often appear on lists of personal goals. We simply assume it will happen. Yet the first rule of friendship should be to assign a top priority to our relationships with others.

If we are to love our neighbors and develop meaningful human relationships, we have to take an interest in them. If we are to be a friend, we have to care about people, about what they think and feel, and about their trials and successes. Friendship is a kind of circle. It cannot enclose the good points without also including the bad.

Most often, friendships stumble on the rock of inconvenience. We may have good impulses and the desire for strong relationships with others, but we find it inconvenient to invest in them. We're willing to do generous things as long as they are personally convenient. But friendship is not always convenient. It always requires the giving of oneself.

The basic principles of human relationships include loyalty, supportiveness, frankness, the ability to keep confidences, and a sense of humor. So it is with friendship. The Savior's Sermon on the Mount is largely devoted to those principles. It offers one of the oldest and most enduring rules of human relationships:

Do unto others as you would have others do unto you. (See Matthew 7:12.)

Perhaps in the long run, that is the best definition of friendship. The result will be an improvement of mankind, a higher degree of cooperation between individuals and among neighbors and nations and families.

MOMENTS
OF
BROTHERHOOD

The Bond of Brotherhood

Not long ago a group of American college students arrived in an eastern European city somewhat apprehensive. The country was not known for its political friendliness to the United States, and in addition, there were representatives there from several other countries, some of which also were not particularly friendly to the United States. But the apprehension soon faded. The tentative smiles on the faces of the young Americans were matched by the smiles of the multinational crowd about them. It was an international folk dance festival, and soon the music was playing and the students were dancing.

Though there was no common spoken language, the young dancers from all over the world were soon so intermixed that it was nearly impossible to tell who was from where. Nor did it matter. They were enjoying their common bond and the association as members of the same human family.

They had learned a truth that all of us would do well to keep in mind. Beneath the screaming headlines, the political propaganda, most people are pretty much the same. They help their neighbors, love their children, want to be appreciated, and would like to make the world a little better than they found it.

Today it is important to emphasize our human similarities, because we are rapidly being pulled into what some social scientists call a "global village." Jets move people from one culture to another in a matter of hours. Orbiting satellites send words or pictures to virtually any corner of the earth instantaneously. The barriers of time and space are coming down. Our separate

151

roads are converging, and we must learn to live together on our shrinking planet.

"There is a destiny which makes us brothers," wrote Edwin Markham. "None goes his way alone." We, like the young dancers, need to enjoy each other's company, bury our hatreds, forget our prejudices. Our eternal destiny is to be one in the human family.

Let us work to catch that vision of oneness, to build the brotherhood of man, to build a bond of brotherhood that will bring us together as children of an eternal Father in heaven.

More Alike Than Different

New Zealand is a green land that lay empty long after other lands had been settled. It waited for its first human voice after civilizations elsewhere had come and gone, after Christ had walked upon the earth. It was a pristine jewel where the only sounds were wild wind and wilder water.

Those who found their way here, guided by wind, current, and stars, came for a place to start anew. They included the Maori, who loved the land, traders looking for fortunes, adventurers who sought freedom, and idealists who wished to build utopia. People came from many lands, bringing the color and flavor of their own cultures. They all came because this was the last frontier, the last place to hope. A. R. D. Fairburn wrote:

> They shouted at the floating leaf,
> laughed with joy at the promise of life,
> Hope becoming belief,
> . . . .
> The crag splitting the sky, slowly
> towering out of the sea, taking
> color and shape, and the land
> swelling beyond.[48]

How much the impulse that shaped our two countries, the United States and New Zealand, is alike. It is easy for us to feel kinship with one another. We speak with a common heritage.

But in a world that is shrinking, we must extend this understanding to those who are not like us, who are not tied together by the thread of adventure that carved out new frontiers.

Mankind is more alike than different. We are reminded that no matter what seems to divide us from peoples of other lands, the rifts are superficial. We all have hands that toil and pray and clap for joy. We have faces lined with the cares and joys of ten thousand days. We are born and cry and dream and question. We share, love, marry, have children. We work, and we die. We are alike. Underneath all the superficialities, we are inexorably alike.

That means we cannot dismiss another's burden or walk by, indifferent. We cannot let life revolve around only ourselves or our family or community. Instead, we have to clasp hands and know the thoughts of men and women in other lands. We have to give up selfishness and convenience to reach out and solve our mutual problems.

> Because we are alike:
> We must not exploit, but nurture each other.
> We must not seek differences, but seek solutions.
> We must not turn our backs, but open our arms.

The poet Carl Sandburg wrote:

> There is only one man in the world
> and his name is All Men.
> There is only one woman in the world
> and her name is All Women.
> There is only one child in the world
> and the child's name is All Children.

E Pluribus Unum

On the great seal of the United States and on our coins is our national slogan: "E Pluribus Unum," which, translated, means "from many, one." Our various histories, heritages, cultural and ethnic diversities intertwine in this land to create the

153

unique character that is an American. How does this happen? How do so many backgrounds blend into so strong a national union?

Some have suggested that the attraction of America is strictly economic. The poor and outcast flee to these shores only for material gain and America's riches. But if wealth were the only magnet, then greed for the goods of this world would immediately divide Americans into thousands of factions as they hungrily and selfishly gather the gold they came for.

Others suggest that America's free business and political climate attracts foreigners. Surely, the blessed freedom of America's Constitution is a treasure beyond price to all who are privileged to live under it. But political and economic freedom alone would also divide Americans, not bind them together. Many from foreign shores have forsaken their own advantage and position to contribute to the common good of America. What, then, is the power that pulls us together?

Sydney Harris suggested that America is not so much a nation as it is an idea. The idea is that "the people are in charge of their rulers and not the other way around."[49] These rights of free agency are God-given to every people, for, as Thomas Jefferson wrote in the Declaration of Independence, "All men are created equal." This belief in equality has stimulated a unifying spirit in America that goes beyond and below our differences of nationality, wealth, creed, or color.

Although we have not yet totally achieved the ideal of equality for all people, it has ever been before us as a beacon, reminding us that we are all brothers and sisters in the family of God.

This enlightened view of responsibility for each other and equality before God is the secret of America's greatness. In the earliest years of our republic, French philosopher Alexis de Tocqueville observed that goodness was the glue holding this diverse nation together. He wrote, "America is great because she is good. And if America ever ceases to be good, America will cease to be great."[50]

Then, as now, of course, Americans were not perfect. There were those, and are those, who would take unfair advantage of this spirit of brotherhood to advance their own selfish interests. But in the main our national treasure of good will to all people, of individual human rights, has been sustained and replenished in war, in peace, in prosperity, and in depression, through hard times and good times.

And so long as we feel love and concern for each other and a reverence for the God and Father of us all, this great nation shall stand strong, and we will continue to be so many voices who sing America's song.

Lives That Touch

More than a century and a half ago, on the American frontier, a young widow stood inside a rough-cut log cabin. She was heartsick. She had been led to believe that the widower she had just married was a man of some means. Now she found herself in conditions of abject poverty. She wanted to run from that sad place; but her eye caught sight of a small boy huddled in a corner in the cabin — very much in need of a mother. The woman, Sarah Bush Johnston, said, "I will stay for the sake of the boy." She stayed and touched his life. Later, that same boy, grown to manhood, touched the lives of millions. He removed the blight of slavery from this land of the free. He helped save America from self-destruction in a civil war — for the small boy was Abraham Lincoln. He would later say of this loving woman, who joined her life with his, "All that I am and all that I ever hope to be, I owe to my angel mother."

"No man is an *Island,* entire of it self," wrote John Donne; "every man is a piece of the *Continent.*"[51] Each of us touches other lives for good or for ill. None of us lives life in isolation. We are born bone of bone and flesh of flesh of our parents. We are immediately and thereafter dependent upon others for food, clothing, shelter, protection, knowledge, and love. None of us could survive singly, and few of us try. We have all been affected by teachers, neighbors, friends, or acquaintances.

That has always been the case. And today's communication and transportation facilities have made us even more aware of our interdependence. Individuals, families, cities, countries, and nations: we are all intertwined with one another on this planet.

The actions of each of us create rippling waves that could quickly spread beyond the horizon of our consciousness and create effects we may never see.

All of us touch other lives every day and leave them better or worse for that contact. Our touch may be as brief as a passing smile or as permanent and profound as the relationship between a parent and a child. But none of us passes through this world without affecting others and being affected by them. The influence we have on others will be the most important and permanent effect we will have in the world.

So let us resolve today to be more aware of the debt we owe to those who have touched our lives. And let us remember that the only way we can begin to repay our debt to them is to go forth and lift the lives of others.

To Be a Christian

When separated from the complex theologies, the religious jargon, and sectarian interpretations, Christianity is at once the most sublime and the simplest morality. The doctrines, as taught by Jesus, are within the comprehension of anyone. The central creed of Christianity is simply to do good — to do good whenever, wherever, and to whomever we can. That is to be a Christian.

It is to believe that feeding the hungry is more important than religious ritual and repetition. It is to match deeds to thoughts, placing human service above lip service, making our home, our office, our neighborhood the production lab for Christian ideals.

To be a Christian is to live with gratitude, with empathy, with gentleness and faith; to seek refinement rather than extravagance; to be worthy before popular; to prefer intrinsic beauty over faddish style.

We will find the Christian wherever there is human need: mowing the lawn of an injured neighbor, standing watch over the sickbed of children, offering a loan to lighten the load of a worthy friend. We will discover his outstretched arms about the huddled shoulders of the mother who has lost an infant to crib death, of the new divorcee who is afraid of the world and of the future, of the boy who sat out the whole game on the bench.

The Christian is made up of the charity that gives without looking back, the humility that kneels when no one is looking, and the faith that believes when the evidence casts doubt.

The Commandments, the parables, and the Beatitudes are written not only in the Christian's Bible and hymnbook but also upon the fleshy tablets of his heart, where they are used for reference. For the true Christian is a person not only of theory but also of application. The first rule of negotiation in business dealings is the Golden Rule. Law is used to gain justice, not money. Peace is made at home as well as at sporting events. And marriage is based on the Christian ideals of equality and mutual respect.

The true Christian is a follower in word and deed of him who became the servant of all: majesty in homespun clothing, manhood tempered by tears, royalty beneath a crown of thorns. Like the silent candle that glows on through the night — quietly, graciously, freely shedding its light — the Christian lives on, grateful for the life that now is and for the promise of that which is to come.

Beyond the Headlines

There was a time when a man knew his neighbors, when all the people in a village or hamlet were known by their first names; a time when news of births and deaths, sickness and good fortune was passed from mouth to mouth, house to house, until all reveled in the joy or grieved in the sadness.

And when the church bells published the news of some departing soul, all stopped to ask for whom the bells tolled; the plowman in the field brought his team to a standstill to count the rings, which tolled the age of him or her whom death had taken from them, alike the housewife at her bread, the carpenter in his shop, the blacksmith at his anvil — all deciphering the mournful message of the bells; one knell — a baby, stillborn in the house by the mill; a dozen tolls — a young boy has drowned in a boating accident; four score—and the soul of the venerable hamlet judge has winged its way to heaven.

But that was then, and this is now. Our modern world is larger, more complex. The printed and electronic news media have replaced the bell tower. We know more about what happens in our world, but distance separates us from the emotional effect of tragic events. We sit quietly in the comfort of our armchair and read the headlines: half a world away a volcano has swept a few dozen villages and twenty thousand inhabitants from the face of the earth. Or we watch on the screen as starving children huddle together to wait for death's calming mercy. Then as casually we turn the page of the newspaper or flip the television channel to catch the football scores or amuse ourselves as make-believe actors perform make-believe tragedies on a make-believe stage.

And so on we go, informed and enlightened but untouched by the news: so and so is dead; we hardly knew him. A town we've never been to with a foreign-sounding name has sunk beneath a sea of suffocating mud, without even a bubble rising to tell its drowning pang. A distant nation of remote peoples whom we've never met starves to death for want of bread.

But there at the scene, where headlines turn to life, some heart has sunk under the weight of the news, a heart close to the misery and death, close to where the tragic news is distilled, to where each ink blot of the printed news and every inch of video is baptized with some mother's tears, close to where every last sensational image represents the agonies and dying groans of real men and women.

May God grant us the empathy to see beyond the headlines: to comprehend more than names and facts; to translate grief-laden news into human terms, making each casualty our neighbor and every victim our brother.

Sharing Life

"Share all of life's joy and be rarely alone, / For exile is empty, a harp without tone."[52] These words by John Colman remind us that we are at our best and happiest when we are with someone else, particularly those we love. In the biblical account of the earth's beginnings, the Lord created the first human being and then pronounced a basic truth: "It is not good that the man should be alone," and he gave Adam, Eve. (Genesis 2:18.)

What was true then is true today. It is not psychologically healthy nor productive nor desirable to live our lives in loneliness. Has not each of us at one time or another seen some beautiful sight or experienced some exciting event and immediately wished our loved ones could enjoy it with us? This desire to blend our lives with others' is as natural to a human being as taking the next breath. We were born to share, to love, to cooperate, to help one another.

As our world continues to get more complicated, more automated, and more technical, there is a danger that we may lose the personal and the human touch that makes our daily activities worth doing. By sharing ourselves with others whom we can help and encourage, we counteract the dehumanizing aspects of a highly technical world. Giving our time, our energies, our attention to others is the most precious gift we can offer. Emerson said, "The only gift is a portion of thyself."

Giving of ourselves, sharing our lives and experiences, is the only way we can build bonds of love to withstand the powerful forces that are isolating people, cultures, and nations today.

Giving financial aid or technological assistance can help improve the lives of others, but sharing ourselves multiplies the effectiveness of our charity.

Caring for and sharing with our brothers and sisters in the human family will help bring peace to this world and prepare us to be worthy of the heavenly world to come.

James Russell Lowell described, from the Lord's perspective, the difference between giving and sharing in these famous lines from *The Vision of Sir Launfal:*

> *Not what we give, but what we share —*
> *For the gift without the giver is bare.*
> *Who gives himself with his alms serves three —*
> *Himself, his hungering neighbor, and me.*

159

The One and the Ninety-Nine

The Savior gave a telling parable when he asked, "What man of you, having an hundred sheep, if he lose one of them, doth not leave the ninety and nine in the wilderness, and go after that which is lost, until he find it?" (Luke 15:4.) Most of us probably wonder about the wisdom of chasing after the one and ignoring the ninety-nine. What happens to the unprotected flock while the shepherd searches?

Yet this simple story tells us as much about the Lord as does a lifetime of experience. Stephen R. Covey said, "Going after the one 'lost sheep' results not in neglecting the 99 but in effectively reaching them."[53]

Why? Think back to the last time someone in your company was critical of another. Recall a moment when a colleague seemed warm and caring to his fellow worker, then turned on him as he moved out of earshot. Did you ever feel as safe in that person's company again, as willing to expose your vulnerabilities? When someone is critical of another, a doubt creeps upon us. We wonder if, when we are gone, he will be critical of us, too, focusing on frailties we know too well but hope others can't see. Such is the point of the parable. Caring for the one shores up trust in the others and gives them confidence in the shepherd, even when he is gone.

That's the way of the Lord. He who knows us best loves us most, even when we feel wayward and worthless, even when we feel undeserving. And who among us never feels like the one left out from a world that seems confidently passing us by?

An important executive confided to a friend that he wondered if his work was worthwhile, if all the time and effort he gave his job counted for anything. If the seemingly confident and powerful feel that way, what about the rest of us? It is so easy to question our worth, our lovability. Self-worth and confidence ebb and flow like a restless wave.

That is why we need the Lord. That is why we can understand more fully the attraction of the Lord's dwelling, why we would rather be a doorkeeper there than enthroned anywhere else. It is because there we feel fully loved, the self-doubts that shadow our lives banished by the light of God.

And so again, the lesson of the parable, whether we dwell with the ninety and nine or are the one, we are assured that when we feel most lost, when we feel tossed about by a buffeting world, the Lord will drop all to come for us.

And we can test the Lord's own principle by using it. "Think about the one," says Covey, "talk to the one, regard the one, serve the one. If you are sincere and constant, you will discover that gradually your influence with the many will be magnified."[54]

A Ballad of Brotherhood

One of the most persistent poetic themes is the brotherhood of man, the responsibility we have to love one another. The result of that love is beautifully expressed by the English Romantic poet Percy Bysshe Shelley: love results in affection that endures, affection that lives after us in the objects of our love.

Indeed, the result of brotherhood and sisterhood is neither temporal nor temporary; it is eternal in both its joy and its power. Nor is such love merely a poetic convention; it is a scriptural truth. The Savior taught us to "love one another," even as he loves us. He called this a "new commandment," not because love is new, but because Christian love is all encompassing. (John 13:34.) No longer can we love them that love us and hate them that hate us. As Christians, the responsibility of our faith is to recognize the common ancestry of all mankind, the brotherhood that binds us all.

True, we come from separate cultures. We have unique customs and traditions. The shape of our eyes may vary, and the color of our skins. But beneath these variations beats a common soul, a bonding more significant and eternal than any apparent separation. We are, in fact, brothers and sisters, and it is our responsibility to love one another.

The Savior made no exception to this exhortation. As God made us all, he made us all to be his children. And we cannot

161

be his children without accepting those brothers and sisters whom he gave us to love. This is the brotherhood of man, and it is through this bonding love that we discover the fatherhood of God and his love for us all.

Roses die, but their fragrance endures. Voices fade, but music continues. And each of us one day shall return to him who gave us life, as surely as the family of which our love is a part shall live forever.

Two Inspiring Invitations

"Come follow me." These welcoming words from Jesus brought a better life and a brighter hope to the discouraged and downtrodden of his day, and they have done the same for millions more in the centuries since he spoke that invitation.

There is another invitation from a different time that has also brought hope to those who suffer in poverty, prejudice, and bondage. It is the one engraved on the base of the Statue of Liberty: "Give me your tired, your poor, your huddled masses yearning to breathe free, the wretched refuse of your teeming shore. Send these, the homeless, tempest-tossed to me. I lift my lamp beside the golden door." Like the words of Jesus, these words have also invited people to change their lives and destinies.

Many who followed the Christ believed the rewards would be worth the price and knew there would be a cost associated with their discipleship. Likewise, those who cast their fate and future with this land of freedom find that freedom isn't free. Happiness isn't handed out, and even the golden door is a door of opportunity that must be pushed open.

The Founding Fathers pledged their lives, their fortunes, and their sacred honor so that we who followed would have an opportunity to pursue happiness. Whether we find it is up to us. And so, both invitations require something more than just wanting to be free, and happy, and blessed. Desire, faith, and hard work are necessary.

Jesus said to his disciples, "Ye are the light of the world." (Matthew 5:14.) Here again is a similarity to the promise of

America. The lamp lifted by that golden door is not a single torch atop a statue. That is only the symbol, the symbol of a combined flame of millions of Americans lifting a light of hope to the world to join with us in pursuing freedom and dignity for all mankind.

Perhaps in the last analysis the two invitations are one. Jesus said, "I am come that they might have life, and that they might have it more abundantly." (John 10:10.) No people in history has ever savored such an abundant life as Americans have. But more than material prosperity are the love of God and the respect for one another that are essential to any successful society. These are the services and sacrifices required of those who would follow Jesus, and they are the same works that will keep the torch of liberty burning brightly in this blessed land.

Who Is My Brother?

The scriptures teach us that we are responsible to love one another, to care for one another, to be brothers and sisters to one another. For, as the apostle John taught, "He that loveth not his brother whom he hath seen, how can he love God whom he hath not seen?" (1 John 4:20.) But it may be even more difficult today than it was in John's day to carry out the scriptural admonition to love one another.

Through most of the world's history, people have lived not knowing the world beyond their homes, acquainted only with the members of their community. But today we hear of the joy and suffering of people throughout the world. Publications, radio, and television tell us about the living and the dying of people we will never meet. Indeed, our lives are so full of information that we may be tempted to ask, "Who is my neighbour?" (Luke 10:29.)

Christ's answer to that question was the parable of the Good Samaritan: "Which now of these," he asked, "was neighbour unto him that fell among the thieves?" The answer: "He that shewed mercy on him." (Luke 10:36–37.)

So it is with us. Our increased knowledge is not only an

increased responsibility but a revelation. For the first time in the history of the world, our media technologies teach us how close we are, how responsible to one another. And our knowledge of our fellowman teaches us how deeply we are brothers, how completely we share a neighbor's responsibility, however separated we may be by geography.

The poet Walt Whitman wrote: "In the faces of men and women I see God . . . , / I find letters from God dropt in the street, and every one is sign'd by God's name."[55]

We are the children of God, each of us, however distant we may be. We are brothers and sisters, the whole world of us. And we have only to believe this for the words of the prophets and poets, and the peace they promise, to come true.

MOMENTS
WITH
THE SAVIOR

"What Think Ye of Christ?"

As another year begins, we experience the annual ritual of examining our priorities and objectives. We often feel the need for more meaning and direction in our lives. There's a desire to increase our spirituality and religious commitment, to bring Christ more into the center of our lives.

Our conscience reminds us of the Savior's powerful teachings—of his admonition to love and serve our fellowmen, not as others do but with a love that far transcends conventional love. If we love only those who love us, he said, what do we do more than others do? He said we must love even those who don't love us and go far beyond. In fact, he told us to acquire the kind of love that he had. That, he emphasized, is the distinguishing Christian personality: "By this shall all men know that ye are my disciples, if ye have love one to another." (John 13:35.)

He constantly urged people to believe in him, to trust in God. He also emphasized over and over again that great things can be accomplished with faith. In Matthew 9:29 we read, "According to your faith be it unto you." In Mark 11:24 we're told that faith can move mountains: "Therefore I say unto you, What things soever ye desire, when ye pray, believe that ye receive them, and ye shall have them." The Lord also made it clear to us that "all things are possible to him that believeth." (Mark 9:23.)

As another new year unfolds, let us practice the principles of love and faith and obedience that the Master taught. Let us ponder his life and respond to his call for action. Let us realize that it's impossible to be indifferent to him, or even neutral. Let us realize that as we lose our lives for his sake, we will find our own true life. We'll discover new depths of happiness and fulfillment that we never knew existed. We'll be forced to admit that he came into the world that we might have life more abundantly.

Ultimately, the choice is ours of whether or not to make Christ a part of our lives. "What think ye of Christ?" was the question put to a group of Pharisees nearly two thousand years ago. (Matthew 22:42.) It was the most vital, the most far-reaching query in an unsettled and distracted world. It is equally important today.

The Light of Christ

There is in each of us a desire to do good — to be good. We love and are loved; we hope for the future; we learn from the past. In every thoughtful, charitable act we perform, in every pleasure we receive from doing good, there is evidence of the goodness in us.

And there is also an evidence of our purpose in the world. Consistent with our natures, we are born into the world to do good, to be good, to make the world a better place, and, in the process, to refine ourselves.

The impulse toward good springs not only from our own eternal natures but also from the Light of Christ, a light that permeates the world, touching and influencing all things, a light that calls all of us to return to a loving Father in heaven who gave us life.

But though the Light of Christ is in each of us and shines through us to the world, there are many in whom this goodness is dimmed — clouded by what they do and by what they fail to do. The agency we have to choose means we are free to choose — free to choose even against ourselves; free to choose against the truth that is in us. And when we choose to do evil, to look away from goodness, a mist settles between us and the light. Just as we are not infallible, neither is the goodness in us infallible — it must be protected to stay bright.

The good work of God is a sweet work. It is the work for which we were born. It is a work designed to help us be better than the world, a work that makes the world better because of us and the good we do. We know this; in the marrow of our bones, we feel this; and we are drawn to it by all that we love and by all of those who love us. We are drawn to it by the Light of Christ that is in us to inspire us, to direct us, to bind us one to another in love, and, ultimately, to call us home.

Triumphal Entry

Jerusalem stirred with passion that Sunday before the Passover. Travelers had clustered there, bringing sacrificial lambs. Coins clattered in coffers where pigeons were sold, and in the temple yard, merchants were busy earning silver from the celebration. But above the hubbub hung a question, Would the prophet from Galilee come? "What think ye, that he will not come to the feast?" they asked one another. (John 11:56.)

Even as they wondered, Jesus Christ's apostles had fetched him a young donkey for his entry into the city. It was to be his last, and so he paused for a moment at the Mount of Olives, looking across at the golden city, and he wept, not for himself, though he knew his death was imminent, but for Jerusalem, a city whose walls and children would be ground into the earth. Then he proceeded.

Word spread that he was coming, and as he rode toward the city, the babble of voices united into an uproar of adulation. "Hosanna to the Son of David," they cried. "Blessed is he that cometh in the name of the Lord." (Matthew 21:9.) Even before he reached the gates of the city, crowds were thronging the way, waving palm fronds and myrtle, spreading their garments in his path. They were giving him a messianic welcome. For this moment, at least, they were his people and he was their king. He came not with armies but riding a gentle animal, and they believed they adored him.

Where was this crowd just five days later when Jesus hobbled to Golgotha, bent under a cross? History does not tell us. Their shouts had been carried away on the wind, their palm fronds withered, and Christ went alone to be crucified.

As we contemplate a lonely Savior on a hillside cross, we may feel critical of this crowd whose love was so brief, but it should teach us something deeper. It is a human tendency for even the most righteous enthusiasm to wane. We are inspired, see with clarity, and then the fog rushes in. We seek to proclaim our love of the Lord, and then circumstances teach us forget-fulness. We mean to amend our character, and then the urgency leaves. We shout for the Lord one day and turn our backs the next. When we hope that we would have rushed out to carry his cross, we need to examine whether even now our shouts swell and ebb on a fickle wind.

His Yoke Is Easy

To enjoy the gift of freedom, the gift of free agency God has given us, we must learn to understand this simple gift of life.

Much has been said and done in this world regarding man's philosophies and theories about our politics and religions; but, after twenty centuries of trial and error, of war and contention, we return again to the wisest, most practical, and simplest system of all. We turn to the gospel of Jesus Christ—to the simplicity of the Sermon on the Mount, to the beauty of the Beatitudes, to the freedom of righteousness. In a very simple way, without money or worldly power, he showed us the path to happiness and eternal life. In his few words and in the sublime gentleness of his life, he offered us a better, clearer, and more intelligent system for individual happiness and social prosperity. While oth-ers talked of governments and laws, of money and influence, Jesus spoke the simple language of the heart. He spoke of loving one's neighbor, of taking care of widows and orphans, of visiting the sick, the elderly, and the imprisoned. He said it is hate that makes life difficult and greed that makes the day hard; he taught of the need to be beautiful within—to have a loving heart, to forgive those who have wronged us, to practice virtue and patience.

To this divine philosophy of life, he added this brief postscript: "Take my yoke upon you, and learn of me. . . . For my yoke is easy, and my burden is light." (Matthew 11:29–30.)

And so it is. Accepting and living the gospel of Jesus Christ is easy—easy if we are Christians in the sense that he wanted us to be; easy if we seek internal refinement over external fashion and wealth; easy if worthiness is more important to us than fame; and easy if we love without condition or reward.

Taking upon ourselves his yoke, or accepting his gospel, may not change the whole world, but it will change our hearts: not that there be no suffering but that suffering might be endured; not that there be no tears but that our tears be mixed with the tears of those who share our hurt or joy; not that there be no mortal death but that the promise of eternal life might live within us.

And thus we take upon us his name and live a life of gentle meekness and charity. It is then we learn of the gift to be simple, the gift to be free. It is then we learn to our joy that his promise is true and his yoke is easy.

The Message of Christ

There are many things the Savior taught us about life and living that are as appropriate today as they were when he walked the shores of Galilee. When Christ described the good life for mankind, his description was of something deeper than the mere pursuit of pleasure and material things. Of greater value, he said, are humility, justice, mercy, compassion, and service—all based on love of God and love of fellowman.

He was acutely aware of the role of money in the lives of the people he taught. He was not opposed to private ownership of property or to the normal process of making a living. But he did warn us of the danger of letting our loyalty and energy be devoted too strongly to money, property, and wealth. He saw danger in the obsession of money—not only because of what it might do to us but also because of what it would do to our relations with others. He reminded us that the number one objective in our lives should be the pursuit of God's will, not for his sake but for ours.

The Savior was a teacher and preacher who knew our physical needs well. He knew that a diseased and suffering body can weaken a healthy spirit and, conversely, that a sick spirit can weaken a healthy body.

He taught us about faith, the mainspring of religious action. He spoke of faith, demonstrated faith, and shared his faith.

Jesus made it clear in his teachings that we live in an orderly universe — one of cause and effect, one where we are responsible for our own actions, a world where we reap what we sow.

As we ponder the life of Christ, we may be inclined to ask, "What meaning is there for me in the teachings of Jesus? What claims do they have upon my life? How are they going to affect my future? Do they have any bearing on my profession, on how I use my time, on the kind of person I am?"

The answers to all such questions are found only in practice, only if we allow room for Christ in our hearts. And if we do, it will bring a sense of wholeness and harmony into our lives. It will provide us with a fundamental core that will unify and integrate our spiritual, intellectual, social, and working lives.

Yes, when we understand the message of Christ, we will also discover depths of happiness and fulfillment we never knew possible.

The Greatest Example

If a picture can be worth a thousand words, an example can be worth more than an entire textbook to a teacher. Every effective teacher knows and uses the power of comparisons, analogies, and examples to explain lessons. Example is the best way to teach some principles, particularly in the vital area of human interaction and relationships. What does it mean to be kind, to be forgiving, to be steadfast, honest, true, to be a good neighbor?

These and other lessons of life can best be learned by seeing them in action.

Such were the teaching methods used by the world's master teacher. Jesus constantly called his disciples' attention to the world about them and drew profound principles from everyday events. To illustrate how one should love his neighbor, Jesus told the story of the Good Samaritan and counseled his followers to do as the Good Samaritan had done. To define charity, he referred to a widow placing her small savings on the temple altar for the poor. Her donation, he pointed out, was much more than that of the rich men with their bags of gold. He observed children, with their pure faith and trust, and told us to become like them.

But more powerful than his pointing out others' examples was the example of the life of Christ himself. When he spoke of forsaking worldly things to build the kingdom of God, he had done it. When he taught the need to search out the lost lamb and bring it back to the fold, there stood the outcasts of society he had restored and redeemed. When he told them to care for their future, they saw him weep over the sins of Jerusalem.

Had they been at Gethsemane, they would have seen Jesus willingly shoulder the sins of the world, and perhaps they would have caught a glimpse of the depth of his love for mankind. "Greater love hath no man than this, that a man lay down his life for his friends." (John 15:13.) And at Golgotha, Jesus illustrated supreme compassion when he prayed for his tormentors, "Father, forgive them; for they know not what they do." (Luke 23:34.)

Because Jesus personified the highest principles of human potential, his teachings and example have changed the destinies of men and nations. His light continues to inspire us to make our own lives better and be examples to those around us. "Let your light so shine before men," he said, "that they may see your good works, and glorify your Father which is in heaven." (Matthew 5:16.)

The Perfect Peace

We often are reminded of our need to seek the perfect peace of Christ, to know his teachings, to embrace eternal principles, to practice the spirit of Christianity. Author C. S. Lewis observed that once we have accepted Christianity, we must be constantly reminded of its concepts, that some of its main doctrines must be deliberately held before our minds every day. "That is why," he said, "daily prayers and religious reading and church-going are necessary parts of the Christian life. We have to be continually reminded of what we believe. Neither this belief nor any other will automatically remain alive in the mind. It must be fed. And, as a matter of fact, if you examined a hundred people who had lost their faith in Christianity, I wonder how many of them would turn out to have been reasoned out of it by honest argument."[56] No, he suggested, most people simply drift away.

Once people lose the light of Christ, there is a flatness to their demeanor. They lose the purpose of life, and when they have forgotten the purpose of living, the universe becomes meaningless. Many in the world today are finding that indifference to the Lord or failure to keep his commandments brings inner turmoil, while the "perfect peace" comes from an ever-closing harmony between our conduct and the Savior's teachings.

Those teachings are not meant to burden us but to help us. In inviting us to follow him, he said, "My yoke is easy, and my burden is light." (Matthew 11:30.) To embrace the teachings of Christ requires us to experience a spiritual metamorphosis, a sort of renaissance of the heart. Such change often helps us meet the pressures of life in subtle ways, sometimes in ways that are hard to articulate. But there is a reserve that his principles provide in our lives, a balance that permits us to endure difficulty.

Lastly, we should always remember that the perfect peace of Christ does not dwell in outward things but within the soul. Recall his words as recorded in John: "Whosoever drinketh of the water that I shall give him shall never thirst; but the water that I shall give him shall be in him a well of water springing up into everlasting life." (John 4:14.)

And so our objective is to find the perfect inner peace of Christ, to drink from the well of everlasting life, and to do so every day of our lives.

Continued Celebration

Observers may look at the life of Christ and call it a failed mission—a gift given to humanity and left unwrapped, forgotten under the Christmas tree. His gift was so homely, after all. We like our gifts with glitter and pomp—a promise of easy days—and he gave something far different.

He came to his people to be their Savior, and they rejected him. "This child is not what we expected," they said, "not a mighty hero to topple all our foes."

He proclaimed peace on earth; yet, with atomic weapons poised above our heads and nations torn with unrest, his proclamation rattles in a dry wind.

He taught love, forgiveness, a chance to turn the other cheek; yet, humanity hurries along, imprisoned in self-preoccupation, divided into factions, and suspicious of the outstretched hand.

He endured all things for our souls' sake until even he, the greatest of all, cried out in pain; and still we pursue pleasure and ease and call our lesser burden heavy.

So we look back on that baby born in Bethlehem—that ultimate condescension of God—to come not just to visit but to be one with us and share in mortality, and we wonder. Have his lessons been lost? Is humanity too distracted to see the star or hear the angel chorus? Are we still saying, "There is no room for him at this inn or in this life"?

No! As we look about humanity, we are aware that many still find room, still remember. We do live in an uneasy world where men's and women's hearts sometimes fail them, but all around us we see a continued celebration of the Savior's birth and life.

When the widow finds solace in grief and raises her head to let the Lord bear her sorrow, we remember. When the weak among us are given courage and the strong offer an arm to a brother, we remember. When a wrong is forgiven and anger is answered with peace, when unbearable burdens are lifted through prayer, when we act better than expediency demands and are more generous than obligation dictates, we remember.

Jesus did not come to this earth in vain, nor is he forgotten.

We may not have gone to the stable on that Bethlehem night those many years ago, but we celebrate his life and his unfailing goodness every time we let him be born again in our hearts.

"Come Follow Me"

In December we celebrated the birth of Christ. We praised him. We sang his name. We talked of his teachings and his example. We followed that with our new year's goals. Now, we might ask if the practice of our resolutions includes the spirit we celebrated at Christmas. Will the fulfillment of our goals and resolutions will be guided by his teachings and his instructions to us?

He showed us the way to make our lives happier. He encouraged us with his invitation to "take my yoke upon you, and learn of me. . . . For my yoke is easy, and my burden is light." (Matthew 11:29–30.)

The teachings of the Savior *are* easy. But many of us have difficulty following them, not because his standards are burdensome, or imprecise, or insufficiently defined, but because, as Neal A. Maxwell observed: "Christ's message clearly gets in the way of the easy flow of carnal life, as some mortals would like to live it."[57]

It is true, of course, that patterning our lives after the Savior's does requires self-discipline, but it's not beyond our capacity. And it is true that some sacrifice may be required, but it is no more than the sacrifices we make daily for rewards far less meaningful than those promised by the Lord.

If we follow his guidelines of honesty, integrity, and service, we will find a sense of direction. We will find motivation, growth, and meaning. We will find peace in our hearts and minds. Those who remember the Savior and his gospel enrich their lives and are reassured by the confirming truth of God's goodness.

There is no greater, more promising, more satisfying goal for a new year than to respond to the Savior's invitation to "come follow me."

MOMENTS
OF
LOVE

Love, a Creative Force

Love is the most quietly creative force in the universe. Babies grow up happily, adults achieve crowning glory, and small impressions are transformed into innovative ideas. Without it, infants turn to the wall and die, adults are broken and diminished, and thoughts are stillborn, never to be translated into action. Love is a need so basic, in fact, that we spend most of our lives seeking it and finally judge ourselves on how much we think we're loved.

A talk show host was interviewing a number of guests on the greatest fears they faced. Most spoke eloquently about nuclear war, the depletion of vital energy reserves; but one, an eminent editor, was strangely silent. Finally, he admitted, "What I fear most is not being loved."

If love is so critical to our happiness, then it is interesting that we live in a society where so many of us struggle in that supreme commitment of love—a happy marriage.

Most of us need one other person with whom we feel the inexpressible comfort of acceptance. We want to meet, at the end of a day that has shredded and discouraged us, with someone who can make us whole again. Yet, that relationship is not easy to achieve. Why? It may be that marriage shows us up for what we are. We all live with imperfect people. No one has a spouse who always lives up to expectations. It may be that the illusion that we are the exception, fostered during the first heady moments of romance, is shattered when we realize that we are two different people whose likes and dislikes differ, who do not always see the same way. It may be that, caught in the mundane dailyness of a world that offers not just joy but also frustration, we blame each other.

Yet, despite these obstacles, we can achieve that love in a marriage that endures and blesses. How?

We can talk to each other, move beyond the easy assumption that our spouse should "just know" how we feel, ask questions of the other that say, "I want to share your experiences, see your viewpoint."

We can understand when our spouse is gloomy, short-tempered, sorrowing; we can expect that she'll have problems or he'll have weaknesses and not be thrown by them.

We can pray for and with each other—plead for his well-being, ask the Lord for ways to bless her life.

We can do the little things for one another—remember a favorite food, write a note, indulge a fancy.

Mostly, we can love. And if our spouse does not seem to respond in the way we might hope, the best thing we can do is just keep loving—for love is the most quietly creative force in the universe.

"Love Thy Neighbour"

The greatest commandment given us by the Savior is to love God with all our heart, soul, and mind. (See Matthew 22:37.) "And the second," he said, "is like unto it, Thou shalt love thy neighbour as thyself." (Matthew 22:39.) It was a message the apostles emphasized repeatedly.

The kind of love referred to by the Lord when he said, "Love one another; as I have loved you" is not dependent on certain prerequisites. (John 13:34.) It's not a reward for good behavior, nor should it be selective.

We are urged to go beyond that point—to love those who injure and wrong us, to be decent whether others are decent or not, to exercise good-will whether others do or not. We're told not to let our conduct depend on how others treat us but to keep an independent personality and stick to our own principles of character regardless of how others act. If we do, we will soon

find that love and the Golden Rule will cover every situation —
something that a list of rules for conduct, however long, could
never do.

The point is that we should love all other persons, whether
they merit it or not, whether they reciprocate our love, whether
they have earned it, or whether we are rewarded for it. Inter-
estingly, the person who is most difficult to love often needs love
the most. And it's not enough for us simply to feel love in our
hearts. We have to express it in our actions.

Loving others requires us to feel good about ourselves. Did
he not say, "Love thy neighbour as thyself"? One of the great
discoveries of modern psychology is that our attitudes toward
ourselves are just as complicated as our attitudes toward others,
and just as important. With this in mind, we might interpret
God's commandment to mean, Thou shalt love thyself properly,
and then thou wilt love thy neighbor. Love for ourselves is the
foundation of a brotherly society and individual peace of mind.

Love can't be confined to any particular part of our lives.
It's a light that shines from within. It's an inner attitude that is
all-embracing. It has to be the central and dominant element in
the life of those who would do the will of God.

Love Unstated

A little girl went on a trip with her parents to an expensive
resort. She got new clothes and swimming equipment for the
vacation; they splurged on wonderful meals. But finally, one day,
the little girl was banging on the wall with her foot, next to her
mother. When her mother could stand it no more, she asked,
"Why are you doing that?"

"I just want you to look at me," the child replied in a moment
of utter honesty.

How much of the present misery and confusion of this world
could be eliminated if we realized that what we need is not more
things, not more gadgets that whirr at us and demand fixing, not
more entertainments or more places to go. What we need and

need desperately is for someone to look at us and really see us, someone to regard us and love us.

In some mysterious way we don't even completely understand, love is tangible. Someone doesn't have to tell us he or she loves us in so many words. We cannot, in fact, tell the smallest part of what we feel. But our intent is read in every action and glance, in tone and gesture, in the very atmosphere we carry.

The infant who cannot even understand the language knows his mother loves him. He feels her quiet movements bringing peace into the fearful, hungry world of first life. She, in turn, does not need to be taught to love. There are no Ph.D.'s in life's highest art. She hears the intent inside the cries, strains at every level to read them.

But if we know when we are loved, we don't always recognize when someone is crying out to us because he or she needs love. The pouting teenager, the screaming child who disobeys his parent, the withdrawn adult who seeks relief in self-destruction— all of these may be cries for love.

Sin itself is often the result of unmet need. So let us regard each other with wiser eyes. Those who seem perverse, rebellious, difficult may be those who yearn for love. Their souls are crying out in tones unformed—"look at me."

It is a clamoring, noisy world. If we are to feed each other, we need to set aside some time to focus on each other. "I just want you to look at me," said the young child. She speaks for us all.

The Greatest of These Is Love

Nowhere in sacred literature is the need for love in our lives expressed more beautifully than in the apostle Paul's letter to the Corinthians. (1 Corinthians 13.) He called it charity. Today, we usually call it love.

And so, in reverent paraphrase, we express the need for this basic human value: for the greatest of these is love.

Though we pay our church donations and attend all our religious services, and have not love — it is nothing.

Though we conform to church ritual, and proselyte as missionaries, and bear titles of ecclesiastical power or authority, but do it without love — we are as the empty shells that line the seashore, having the semblance of life but not the spirit.

Though we bequeath our money to great universities and charitable causes; and though magnificent buildings bear our names, monuments our visage, and newspapers our photograph — in the absence of love, we are none the better.

And even if we develop the technology to speed ourselves to the far reaches of the universe, or to peer at the smallest microbe, or to have the knowledge to cure ourselves of all disease and poverty — if love is lacking, it profits us little.

Love is patient and wise — patient with the gentle forbearance that waits on others before itself and wise with the gentle wisdom of old eyes that, having looked on time, know that the simple act of being kind is greater than all the wisdom of the wise.

Love is not boastful nor self-interested but understands that no one has achieved success without the help and sacrifice of others.

Where love is, there also are faith, hope, and endurance. Without love, the richest man is made poor; with love, the poorest man is made rich.

When war is nothing more than a rusting relic of a frightful past; when the gallows and ghettos have crumbled into dust; when the last terrorist, the last tyrant, the last murderer and rapist have crept silently to rest — love will remain, and will rule, because love knows no death.

Fame dies, honors perish, and the worldly hope men set their hearts upon turns to ashes. But love lives on — through decades, through centuries, through eons — for the greatest of these is love.

"Love One Another"

Simple, yet profound; brief, but far-reaching; old, yet ever new — the three words spoken twenty centuries ago by the gentle carpenter from Galilee: "Love one another." (John 13:34.) It is a plain and precious commandment, running like a thread of gold through the long history of mankind, as unchanging and relevant as time itself.

Love one another: because the greatest cause of the world's sorrow is the lack of love.

Love one another: because that person who cannot love is like half a pair of scissors—functionless, missing the essential portion of personality that is divinely human.

Love one another: because those who love do not fear hate; because those who love begin to live; because to love and be beloved are the eternal building blocks of human happiness.

To love one another is to understand one another. It is to realize that regardless of language, customs, mores, or race, all people are basically the same. It is to surmise that our neighbors have the same hurts, frustrations, and intelligence as ourselves.

Imagine a world, a nation, a community, or a family where love rules: a world without war. Imagine nations without border guards: nations spending their resources on food, medicines, education instead of on missiles and bombs.

Think of that community or town where "the greatest good for the greatest number" is the maxim: a place where hatred, bigotry, and prejudice are forgotten terms of a forgotten past.

And picture a family in which love is the motivating force: no child abuse, no neglect, no fighting over inheritance or family possessions; but, in their place, parents who are honored and respected by children, children who demonstrate open affection for each other, grandparents who are revered and attended.

Love is a verb, a word of action—not just something to talk about or feel, but something to do. When we begin to wash each other's feet, when we can safely forget to deadbolt our homes at night, when we no longer have a need for military weapons—then we can say that we love one another.

And so, a revolution is needed—a courageous, boisterous revolution with waving banners and battle hymns, a revolution to overcome intolerance and vengeance, a revolution to triumph over the infectious hatred that cripples our planet—a revolution of the heart. And let this be its motto, its standard, its bill of rights—that we love one another.

Our Savior's Love

We can take great comfort and encouragement in the fact that the primary attribute of God is love. He loves each one of us specifically, individually, and respectively. Yet, living as one of billions on a small globe swimming in a sea of space, we can easily feel inconsequential. Who are we that God should take notice of us? In a world where events seem sometimes random, often frustrating or hostile, it is easy to feel overlooked. Why should our days be numbered before the Lord?

But they are. God does notice us. In the great awesomeness that is the universe, there is a personal concern. As Neal A. Maxwell said: "We are living on a small planet which is part of a very modest solar system, which, in turn, is located at the outer edge of the awesome Milky Way galaxy. If we were sufficiently distant from the stunning Milky Way, it would be seen as but another bright dot among countless other bright dots in space, all of which could cause us to conclude, comparatively, 'that man is nothing.' (Moses 1:10.)

"Yet we are rescued by such reassuring realities as that God knows and loves each of us—personally and perfectly. Hence, there is incredible intimacy in the vastness of it all."[58]

God is perfect in his love. It is not too hard for him who set the worlds in motion, whose understanding pierces the intricacies of physics, mathematics, and astronomy, to have a knowledge that centers on each individual. He can call each of us by name, knows our burdens and joys, is familiar with our past and future.

Remember when he blessed the little children? It was not a blanket blessing, with a wave of his hand on the multitude. He took them to him one by one.

When he looked out upon a multitude, he said, "Have ye any that are sick among you? Bring them hither. Have ye any that are lame, or blind, or halt, or maimed, or leprous, or that are withered, or that are deaf, or that are afflicted in any manner? Bring them hither and I will heal them, for I have compassion upon you; my bowels are filled with mercy." (3 Nephi 17:7.) And he did heal them, one by one, not as a faceless mob.

What does that mean for us in this time? It means we are

not alone in this dangerous mortal journey. It means the Lord does not look on humanity with a kind of general good-will. He looks upon each of us individually with a love whose fullness and intensity we can scarcely comprehend.

Though the whirlwind may blow and the fires rage, though the pain and anguish of life may sometimes threaten to consume our very lives, ultimately we are safe because the Lord loves us. Ultimately, the vast universe is an intimate place, because our Creator makes it so.

On Love

Democracy has a value in our personal lives as well as in our national existence. There needs also to be democracy in our love of others. What seems to be love is often not love at all. In fact, in the name of love, one may do things that hurt or harm another.

Psychiatrist M. Scott Peck reported what one timid young man said: "My mother loved me so much she wouldn't let me take the school bus to school until my senior year in high school. Even then I had to beg her to let me go. I guess she was afraid that I would get hurt, so she drove me to and from school every day, which was very hard on her. She really loved me."[59]

The story reminds us that love is not just a feeling and not even just a series of actions. Love has much to do with the conscious or unconscious purpose in the mind of the lover.

Often, what we call love is the desire to control. We sacrifice for others and become ego-rewarded when they become dependent upon us. These are the people who assume responsibility for everybody else's problems. They may shield their children or their spouse from consequences. They may diminish children by doing for them what they should do for themselves. They may go about seeking to change those closest to them according to a personal formula. The message they are giving, without knowing it, can be painful. In subtle ways, the acts we think we do for love may not have a loving effect at all.

We are reminded that we need to love those we love not just with our hearts but with our heads as well. We need to be judicious and wise. We need to consider them not just as they relate to us but in their own context. How does the world look to them? What are their hopes and dreams? What affirms them?

This means that it is as important to know when to hold back as when to give. It means that we must fiercely guard the agency of those whom we love. We must think of them not just in the way they may satisfy our needs but help them to satisfy their own. We must regard them with the deepest respect.

The Lord has set the pattern. His love for us allows us to be what we are. It would be easier for us sometimes if he did not respect us so much. But his love is not controlling. We suffer the consequences of our own actions. We are not allowed the luxury of childish ways with childish restrictions. His intent, like the intent of those who truly love, is to celebrate the person, celebrate the one you love. And when we can learn to love as he does, there is much to celebrate.

Broadcast Dates

191

Notes

1. In Obert C. Tanner, *Christ's Ideals for Living* (Salt Lake City: Obert C. and Grace A. Tanner Foundation, 1980), p. 56.

2. In *You Can See Forever,* comp. Caesar Johnson (Norwalk, Conn.: C. R. Gibson Co.), p. 9.

3. Ibid., p. 14.

4. Franklin D. Roosevelt, Inaugural Address, 4 Mar. 1933.

5. In Paul F. Boller, Jr., *Presidential Anecdotes* (Oxford Univ. Press, 1981), p. 8.

6. Najile S. Khoury, in Richard L. Evans, *Richard Evans' Quote Book* (Salt Lake City: Publishers Press, 1971), p. 160.

7. James Allen, *As a Man Thinketh* (Salt Lake City: Bookcraft), p. 44.

8. *Tragedy or Destiny,* BYU Speeches of the Year (Provo, 6 Dec. 1955), pp. 4–5.

9. In Evans, *Richard Evans' Quote Book,* p. 130.

10. In Samuel Smiles, *Character* (A.L. Burt Co.), p. 364.

11. *Character,* p. 359.

12. *From Quaker to Latter-day Saint: Bishop Edwin D. Wooley* (Salt Lake City: Deseret Book Co., 1976), p. 174.

13. In Tanner, *Christ's Ideals for Living,* p. 190.

14. In Evans, *Richard Evans' Quote Book,* p. 175.

15. "Choose Something Like a Star," line 25.

16. In Richard G. Capen, Jr., "There's Good News for You," *Vital Speeches of the Day,* 15 Aug. 1983, p. 667.

17. *The Lake Isle of Innisfree.*

18. See "Personal Glimpses," *Reader's Digest,* Sept. 1961, p. 11.

19. Blaise Pascal, *Pensees.*

20. *An Essay on Criticism,* lines 215–16.

21. Neil Postman, "Amusing Ourselves to Death," New York University.

22. *Deseret News,* 25 Sept. 1984, pp. U1–2.

23. See Tanner, *Christ's Ideals for Living,* p. 14.

24. In Tanner, *Christ's Ideals for Living,* p. 15.

25. See Jack Fincher, *The Brain: Mystery of Matter and Mind* (Washington, D.C.: U.S. News Books, 1981), p. 7.

26. *Hymns of The Church of Jesus Christ of Latter-day Saints* (Salt Lake City: The Church of Jesus Christ of Latter-day Saints, 1985), no. 215.

27. Address delivered at American Academy of Achievement, New Orleans, June 1982.

28. In *Leaves of Gold,* ed. Clyde Francis Lytle (Coslett Publishing Co.), p. 36.

29. See *The Screwtape Letters* (Lord and King Associates), p. 119.

30. In Evans, *Richard Evans' Quote Book,* p. 61.

31. *The Problem of Pain* (New York: Collier Books), p. 42.

32. Ibid., p. 44.

33. "To the Virgins to Make Much of Time."

34. *Hamlet,* act 5, scene 1, lines 236–37.

35. "Nothing Gold Can Stay," line 8.

36. Author unknown, "Clouds."

37. *The City of God,* trans. Marcus Dods (New York: Modern Library, 1950), p. 854.

38. James Boswell, *Life of Johnson.*

39. Boyd K. Packer, Apr. 1970.

40. John Greenleaf Whittier, "O Brother Man!"

41. Christopher M. Wallace, "Intimacy," in *Counseling: A Guide to Helping Others,* ed. R. Lanier Britsch and Terrance D. Olson (Salt Lake City: Deseret Book Co., 1985), 2:138.

42. "The Secret of Strong Families," *Ladies Home Journal,* Feb. 1983, p. 62.

43. *Psychology Today,* May 1986.

44. Act 2, scene 2, lines 80–81.

45. *Essays,* II, "Affections of Fathers," p. 8.

46. *The Lay of the Last Minstrel,* canto 6, lines 1–6.

47. *Hymns,* no. 293.

48. In Brian Bate and Maurice Shadbolt, *New Zealand – Gift of the Sea* (Honolulu: East-West Center Press).

49. "What's Happened to Americanism?" *Deseret News,* 3 July 1985, p. 14A.

50. *La Democratie en Amerique,* 1835.

51. *Meditation XVII.*

52. *Life's Joy* (New York: Associated Music Publishers, 1964).

53. *Spiritual Roots of Human Relations* (Salt Lake City: Deseret Book Co., 1970), p. 139.

54. Ibid., pp. 140–41.

55. *Song of Myself,* lines 1285–86.

56. *Mere Christianity* (New York: Macmillan Publishing Co., 1952), p. 124.

57. *Even As I Am* (Salt Lake City: Deseret Book Co., 1982), p. 17.

58. *Ensign,* July 1982, p. 51.

59. *The Road Less Traveled* (New York: Simon and Schuster, Touchstone, 1985), p. 82.

Index